WHAT SHOULD METHODISTS TEACH?

WESLEYAN TRADITION AND MODERN DIVERSITY

WHAT SHOULD METHODISTS TEACH?

WESLEYAN TRADITION AND MODERN DIVERSITY

Edited by

M. Douglas Meeks

KINGSWOOD BOOKS
An Imprint of Abingdon Press
Nashville, Tennessee

WHAT SHOULD METHODISTS TEACH?

WESLEYAN TRADITION AND MODERN DIVERSITY

Copyright © 1990 by Abingdon Press

Library of Congress Cataloging-in-Publication Data

What should Methodists teach? : Wesleyan tradition and modern diversity / edited by M. Douglas Meeks.
      p.   cm.
   ISBN 0-687-44912-X (alk. paper)
   1. Methodist Church—Doctrines.   2. Methodist Church—Teaching office
   I. Meeks, M. Douglas
BX8331.2.w515   1990   262'.8'08827—dc20   90-34123

ISBN 0-687-44912-X

Printed in the United States of America
on acid-free paper

To the memory of
Albert Cook Outler

Contents

Introduction

M. Douglas Meeks

The essays of this book were originally given as papers at the Eighth Oxford Institute of Methodist Theological Studies convened at Somerville College, Oxford, England, in the summer of 1987. The theme of the Institute, "The Significance of Methodist Teaching and Practice for Confessing the Apostolic Faith," emerged out of an historic moment of the church's search for integrity and unity in its teaching. The theme reflects a period in which the churches of the world Methodist and Wesleyan traditions are searching for a fresh approach to the standards of teaching the faith. The question is pressed whether there is a theological consensus in world Methodism about what Methodist/Wesleyan churches should teach and what they should contribute to the *oikumene*. What would it require for these churches to work toward such a consensus on sound teaching and praxis? Are there valid limits of diversity, dissent, and conflict both among and in the Methodist churches?

As it hands on the faith to the next generation of Christians and reformulates it for proclamation and mission to the world, the Church must be clear about the content of its teaching and the ways in which it understands the truth of its teaching. As heuristic principles for studying Methodist consensus on teaching the faith the Institute worked with the questions for the first Methodist Conference in 1744: What to teach? How to teach? What to do? The following essays tend to give differing emphases to these questions. Some stress the content of Christian teaching, some deal with the peculiar difficulties of teaching the faith in modern society, and some focus on the praxis of faith as the key to teaching. Each author, however, comes to grips in his or her own way with several common questions: How are the authority and truth of Christian teaching to be established? In what ways has the authority of Christian teaching been distorted by the dominative ways of thinking and governing in the West and even by the church's own traditions? Is it possible to speak of the unity and truth of Christian teaching in a pluralistic society? Are there new models of unity? Are there new ways of understanding the truth of the faith in face of the all-encompassing exigencies of the human future?

Brian Beck's essay describes the context of this Institute and offers a realistic assessment of the ways in which the worldwide Methodist community of learning can address teaching. Beck argues that all ways of teaching the faith must recognize the particularity of the histories and contexts in which churches live and give witness to the world. The immediate goal of the scholarly community should not be convergence. Rather, teaching that serves the evangelism and mission of the church can lead to unexpected new realities in a richly diverse community.

Albert Outler also takes seriously the reality of dissensus and controversy in this period of the decline of the Enlightenment certainties. But he sees great contemporary relevance in Wesley's recourse to the Christian tradition in its diverse forms for new patterns of Christian unity today. As a crucial step toward consensus among Methodists Outler proposes a critical retrieval of Wesley's focus on the rule of grace through the person and work of the Holy Spirit. This could rescue Methodism from its domestications and provide an ecumenical soteriology of great interest to contemporary people weary of the modern lust after self-salvation.

C. K. Barrett takes a critical look at the biblical grounding of distinctive Methodist teachings on righteousness and justification and ways in which some traditional Methodist teachings might need to be corrected and energized by a critical reading of the scriptures. According to Barrett, the justification of sinners by grace through faith should remain the key to Methodist teaching.

G. R. Evans traces the great debates on consensus and dissensus in church teaching during the Reformation period as a background to Wesley's own search for a faith that has been held by all Christians everywhere and at all times. Is Christian truth essentially fixed? What part is played by the imaginative power of interpretation in the reception of the faith passed on? How can we be certain of the truth of the Apostolic faith and that we have truthfully interpreted it?

These questions do not belong only to the dusty past. They are very much alive in ecumenical theology today. Günther Gassmann provides an analysis of the process of the World Council of Churches study "Towards the Common Expression of the Apostolic Faith Today," which has caught the imagination not only of the Orthodox and the Roman Catholics but also of Christians from the developing world. Geoffrey Wainwright proposes several ways in which Methodism can both benefit from and contribute to the WCC project. He demonstrates how Wesley's teaching was constitutively ecumenical and can be a model for our attempt today to hold together the confession of the one gospel in diverse contexts of the world.

It is becoming increasingly clear that Christian teaching today must be done in the face of radical diversity of cultural, socio-economic, political, and religious contexts. Several essays in this volume view the question of pluralism as the most thorny issue regarding the content, method, and authority of Christian teaching. José Míguez Bonino asks how the church can teach universally on the questions of human survival which have become global when in a pluralized world almost everything the church says seems controversial. After comparing three different modes of ecclesiastical teaching on social questions, he argues that the assumptions of "liberal pluralism" may not serve the necessity of Christian teaching to choose concrete options in a particular political situation. Mercy Amba Oduyoye paints a vivid picture of the conflict in teaching among, on the one hand, the more traditional churches of Africa shaped by Western missions in which patriarchalism and hierarchalism destroy authority and, on the other hand, the emerging indigenous teaching which gains its authority from its empowering persons for liberation from their oppression. Adrian Hastings examines the situation of Christian teaching in the context of the pluralized university and argues that Christian teaching must have the courage to express its own particularity in a situation in which a misguided search for a universal religion assumes that everything scandalous about the historical reality of the religions can be transcended.

It is a delight to express our gratitude to the many persons and agencies who made the Institute possible. Among those are the Reverend Joe Hale, General Secretary of the World Methodist Council, who was generous in his support. Donald Treese provided valuable advice on many aspects of the Institute's life and work. Financial subvention was provided by the Division of Ordained Ministry of the United Methodist Board of Higher Education and Ministry, the United Methodist Board of Discipleship, the Overseas Division of British Methodism, and the United Methodist Board of Global Ministries. The work of the Institute was greatly enhanced by the creative leadership of the Working Group Conveners: Phyllis Bird and Peder Borgen, Richard Heitzenrater and Thomas Langford, Donald Dayton and Reginald Ward, Philip Wogaman and José Míguez Bonino, David L. Watson and Lawi Imathiu, and Theodore Runyon and Norman Young.

The volume is dedicated to the memory of Albert C. Outler who for many years epitomized the spirit of the Oxford Institute and whose learning, teaching, and vision will surely shape its future service to the people called Methodist and to the *oikumene.*

Chapter 1

PROSPECTS FOR METHODIST TEACHING AND CONFESSING

Brian E. Beck

The original concept of the Oxford Institute of Methodist Theological Studies was that of a gathering of Methodist scholars in the city which was so influential in the lives of John and Charles Wesley and the beginnings of Methodism in order to recover something of our Methodist or Wesleyan identity and explore the received faith together. Over the years the character and focus of the Institute have changed. It has become far more comprehensive in its membership, including more countries of the world, and embracing also those churches and traditions which look to Wesley for their origins and inspiration but distinguish themselves from the Methodist Churches as they are known today. As a consequence it has grown in size. In its tendency the Institute has shifted from being a gathering of Methodists discussing theology to being a gathering of theologians discussing Methodism. The topics of the various Institutes illustrate this: in 1958 "Biblical Theology and Methodist Doctrine," in 1962 the "Doctrine of the Church," in 1965 the "Finality of Christ," in 1969 the "Living God," in 1973 the "Holy Spirit," in 1977 "Sanctification and Liberation," and in 1982 "The Future of the Methodist Theological Traditions." In its style of working, much more emphasis is now placed on group work, each group having its particular program, rather than simply discussing the plenary papers, and a continuity between Institutes has been established with the category of associate membership and the publication of *Oxford Notes*.

This Institute is designed to pick up where its predecessor left off. The structure is constituted by working groups and a distinguished panel of lecturers who will introduce various aspects of the theme, not necessarily tied to one of the group programs, which are relevant to all our work. Our gathering is from some thirty countries, including South Africa and countries in Eastern Europe, and it is good to record our gratitude to the World Methodist Council and to Boards and Divisions in the United States and

Great Britain, which through their financial aid have made so widely representative a gathering possible.

The theme of this Institute is "The Significance of Methodist Teaching and Practice for Confessing the Apostolic Faith." I should like to offer some very general reflections on that theme. Most of what I have to say can be grouped around two words in the title, "Methodist" and "Apostolic."

Let us first turn to the word "Methodist" which reminds us that we are engaged in an exploration of our common identity. We are trying to state who we are. Though almost all of us are representatives of the Methodist/Wesleyan tradition, that is a much more complex fact than we sometimes recognize. It is more accurate to say, for example, that we are representatives of Methodist/Wesleyan traditions; that is, we belong to distinct churches and communities, each of which has its own version of that tradition. And these different versions of the tradition have been formed not only by our common historical origins in the life and work of John and Charles Wesley and our common possession of their writings, but by our very different subsequent histories, from the end of the eighteenth century to today. Those subsequent histories do not just comprise theological developments but a whole host of factors which have made our various churches what they are now. Events in secular history, our social and economic context, our experience of colonialism, or of a dominant Hindu culture, or of slavery, or economic dependence, internal conflict, language barriers, revival movements, to give a few examples, all these have helped to shape what we have become and the way we do things and see things. Our differing theological traditions are in part at least the result of reflection upon what we are, and we shall not understand those traditions without attention to all the factors which have shaped them.

Let us remind ourselves therefore that, like all Christians but more sharply than some, we stand as individuals, each of us in a dialectical relation to our particular church's tradition, partly molded by it, partly critical of it. No one individual wholly represents his or her church. No one individual can do so, or even wholly understand that tradition, for the corporate tradition is wider than the individual.

This is especially true of academics. Most of us who gather here represent at least two traditions: the Methodist/Wesleyan tradition to which we belong ecclesiastically, and the academic tradition, the discipline of study and research in history, theology, Bible, economics, whatever it is, in which we were trained and in which some of us serve professionally. This tradition is international. It has of course its own schools and fashions and variants, but they do not coincide with denominational boundaries. In a gathering like this both types of traditions meet. The Methodist traditions are modified by the academic. Perhaps the academic traditions may be

14

modified by the Methodist, though I think that is less likely. The field of biblical studies is a prime case of what I mean. It is possible that I interpret certain texts in a particular way because I am a Methodist; Romans 7 would be a test case. But I am quite clear that for the most part my teachers are Joachim Jeremias and Ernst Käsemann and Raymond Brown and not John Wesley. That applies to other areas of study as well. In other words we have to remember to ask the question, how representative are we of the Methodist tradition to which we belong?

Then again let us remind ourselves that all our traditions, and all of us as individuals, have been deeply influenced by ecumenical contact and dialogue. There has been cross-fertilization in the last hundred years, which means that the traditions we have today, traditions both of faith and practice, are not just the simple growth of seedlings planted in the eighteenth century, nor just the more complex flowerings of regional varieties produced by the interaction of the original stock with different environments in different parts of the world, but to some extent hybrid things, the product of the interaction of Methodism with the wider church. This has always been true of our hymnody. It is evident nowadays in my own church in the realm of liturgy, and of course in the growing questioning of the doctrine and practice of infant baptism. But then our beginnings also had an ecumenical stamp upon them before we tended to draw into ourselves.

When we talk about Methodist teaching and practice or about the Methodist or Wesleyan tradition, therefore, we are talking about a very varied thing with many manifestations, the product of many influences which is constantly in movement. For every strand of the tradition and for every individual within it there is a tension between past and future, between the direction in which we are moving and the direction in which we ought to move. Each one of us has a question of identity. So our exploration of our common identity involves a search for authenticity. There are ways of expressing our traditions which are true to them and ways that are false; ways of developing those traditions, moving them on, which will fulfill them and enable them to flower, and ways which will distort and deny them. How is authenticity to be judged? Which elements of what we believe and do are to be recognized as truly Methodist, the genuine thing, and which are not?

Some of us, perhaps all, have inherited doctrinal standards, which in some sense or another lay down a norm. For British Methodism they include the first four volumes of John Wesley's *Sermons* and the *Notes on the New Testament.* Wesley chose them himself and laid them upon posterity. Whether that was a wise decision is open to debate, for they are hardly specific enough to serve as a test of authentic Methodism, and I cannot imagine a doctrinal trial, for instance, where the verdict of guilty or innocent would be settled by reference to one of the sermons or Wesley's exposition of a particular verse. The 1932 Deed of Union of the British Church betrays our embarrassment when it says, "The Notes on the New Testament and the 44 Sermons are not intended to impose a system of formal or speculative theology on Methodist Preachers, but to set up standards of preaching and belief which should secure loyalty to the fundamental truths of the Gospel of Redemption and ensure the continued witness of the Church to the realities of the Christian experience of salvation." Looking through the opening pages of the 1984 *United Methodist Book of Discipline* I notice that the problem is not peculiar to British Methodism.

If this is not an adequate test of authenticity, what is? Is there some other "canonical" or "normative" point of reference? Are there other particular Wesleyan writings? Is there a golden age in our history, to which we can look back as giving us the key, the test, for the authenticity of our Methodism today? In popular thought it is often the teaching and example of John Wesley himself. Fairly often I get letters in my office pointing out that if only the Methodist Church in Great Britain returned to the teaching and evangelical zeal of John Wesley, Britain would be converted once again. But as our historians are always pointing out, such an ideal of John Wesley is highly selective. My correspondents, for example, do not intend modern Methodism to return to horse riding or experiments with electricity. No alleged golden age is uniformly gold. And if, as our historians insist, we add the later Wesley to the earlier, the problems get worse. Not every development in Wesley's thought, surely, was necessarily an improvement, nor, on the other hand, necessarily a sign of senile decline. So by what are we to be guided? And when we remember that the later Wesley sometimes republished earlier works unedited alongside later writings with a different slant, our difficulties increase. But why should Wesley provide the golden example? Or why Wesley alone? Why should authentic Methodism be judged by the eighteenth century rather than the nineteenth or twentieth?

Does this mean that the search for authenticity is futile? That there can be no authentic Methodism but only undifferentiated manifestations of Methodism? Can we do no more than ask of any new development, in belief or practice, whether it has happened before? Can we go no further than legitimization by precedent? This was a point forced upon me in a recent project where we were exploring ways in which we could restructure our annual Conference. It was easy to find historical precedents for the changes we were considering; it was harder to show that they were precedents which deserved to be followed. One answer to our problem (and here especially the systematic theologian has a part to play) is to introduce the notion of coherence. What are those features of the Methodist movement, the concepts, the ideas, the practices, which are typical of it, which tend to persist with the passage of time and somehow account for other features? On the other hand, what are the features which are merely incidental, which could be lost or jettisoned without damage or distortion? If we could detect a web or network of central features which supported each other, which cohered with each other in an intelligible pattern, it might be possible to develop a test for authenticity. We could ask of any modern development in doctrine or practice whether it cohered with this central core, whether logically, naturally, theologically, it followed from it, belonged to it, could be fitted into it, or whether it had to be seen as an alien intrusion, even a contradiction.

A final point to make in this little discussion of authenticity is that judgements about what is authentic in our tradition cannot be taken simply by reference to the past, nor are they simply intellectual judgments. To discern what is authentic in the tradition is a judgment of today's church, a collective response, in which the church of the past in its historical context, with all the limitations that implies, speaks to the church of today, to us, in our context, with all our limitations, and offers us insight, stimulus, and challenge for our life and work; and we recognize its authenticity because in our situation it "fits." To discern authenticity is a gift of the Holy Spirit, the interpreter of the past, who illuminates the present with the truth of God.

There is one other point to address before we leave the general topic of the search for identity. It is sometimes assumed that in a gathering like this we are looking for a Methodist convergence. We come with our various versions of the Methodist inheritance. How close are we seeking to bring them together? Can we look for a doctrinal statement of World Methodism, a formulation of the faith which will bring together all our different varieties in a single blend and somehow supersede them, so that in the future we may all speak with one voice? We have one recent example of that in the World Methodist Statement "Saved by Grace," the so-called Jerusalem Statement. Can we go beyond that and work out a common position in more detail? Is there a World Methodist gospel? This is an attractive proposition. It would make international confessional dialogues much easier if we did not have to qualify almost every statement by pointing out the differences in our own ranks. But I doubt whether it is possible, or really desirable, precisely because we come from so many different settings and have been shaped by such different histories. As I shall want to emphasize again shortly, our task is not to formulate a doctrinal position for its own sake, but to address our particular contexts in the name of Christ. Since those contexts differ, our expression of the faith must also differ if we are to address the world from where we are.

The goal of our discussions is not Methodist convergence, still less uniformity, but mutual enrichment. The emphasis in some parts of the world, for example, on the gospel of and for the poor should alert us all to the presence of that concern in our common tradition and the need of it for all of us in our different settings if we are to witness to the gospel in its wholeness, even if we give expression to it in different ways.

So far we have been looking at a group of issues raised for us by the presence of the word "Methodist" in our title, "The Significance of Methodist Teaching and Practice for Confessing the Apostolic Faith." Now we turn more briefly to a cluster of thoughts which gather around the word "Apostolic."

Our title was deliberately chosen, not just as a test of how many words you can say without drawing breath, but because it echoes the theme of the World Council of Churches' Faith and Order program, "Toward the Common Expression of the Apostolic Faith." Our work is designed as a contribution to a wider ecumenical dialogue. The reality of that wider setting is brought home to us in the Institute in other ways also, by the presence of ecumenical observers from the Church of England, the Roman Catholic Church, and the United Reformed Churches, by the reports we shall receive on bilateral dialogues, and by the contributions of Dr. Günther Gassmann of the World Council of Churches and Professors Adrian Hastings and Gillian R. Evans.

It is vital that we should have this wider setting if we are to get a true perspective of ourselves. We are not the whole embodiment of the church of Christ, and our understanding of the gospel is not a total understanding. To imagine otherwise or to think that we alone were the true church would be to retreat into sectarianism.

It is important to set our conversations in a wider framework also because it is in the questions and comments which others put to us that we are enabled to see ourselves more clearly. The questions I have tried to raise about the Methodist traditions, about diversity and identity and authenticity, are the questions that have to be resolved with regard to ecumenical diversity and catholic identity and authenticity among all the Christian traditions. It is at least as hard to decide what is "apostolic" as to decide what is Methodist. Reflecting on these questions in one setting is likely to help our reflection in another.

I draw attention, however, particularly to the word "confessing," "confessing the apostolic faith." It points to two types of activity, although of course they are linked. On the one hand, there is worship. The faith is confessed when we worship God (Heb. 13:15), affirm the creed, declare the wonderful deeds of him who brought us out of darkness into light (1 Pet. 2:9), baptize, and celebrate the Eucharist. Faith itself is a confession of the

18

glory of God (Rom. 10:9ff.). The other kind of confession, of course, is in witness to the world, the willingness, whatever the cost, to speak and live in such a way that the gospel is made known. The "confessors" *par excellence* have been those who have been willing to lay their lives on the line rather than deny the faith by which they live.

"Confession" is a word which joins together word and action in an obedient declaration to the world of the God we worship. If we discuss confessing the faith in this Institute, then we cannot confine ourselves to the formulation of doctrine. We must also talk about prayer and living and mission and evangelism. All alike are modes of confessing the faith.

Let us come to this same point by a more Methodist route. In 1744 John Wesley and a tiny handful of friends held the first Methodist Conference. There were three items on the agenda: What to teach, How to teach, What to do? Those men also were engaged, like us, in a search for identity. They were engaged in controversy with others on important doctrinal issues. They were attacked by detractors. They were working for the most part separately and needed to know where they stood, and where those who might join them would be standing, too. But the questions they asked were intensely practical questions. They were doctrinal issues about justification and quietism and the established church, but they had a missionary slant. It was not "What to believe" but What, and How, to teach, and What to do, How to regulate the common life of those who respond to the teaching. These were men under compulsion: they had been taken over by a deep conviction of the grace of God and were under obedience to live out its implications and proclaim it for others. Their conference had a clear evangelistic and missionary emphasis.

It is in keeping with this that our Institute theme refers to Methodist teaching and practice, and (in the missionary sense of the word apostolic) to the apostolic faith. We should keep ourselves in that dimension, so that living and doing, evangelism and mission, in short the praxis of the apostolic faith, is the thrust of all our work. What are the implications of our work for our preaching and our living, our service, our engagement in conflict, our prayer?

These remarks may help to give a setting for the work of the six groups. For the first time a group is dealing specifically with biblical issues. In earlier Institutes there was a period of Bible study for all at the beginning of the day. It never seemed to be very successful, partly because people came with different expectations and levels of preparedness, partly because it was difficult to integrate the studies with the theme of the Institute as a whole. This time there is a group to work on specific biblical questions. It is obvious why it is needed. When one considers how not only the Wesleys but all their successors throughout the nineteenth century at least founded their work on biblical texts, it is important to ask how far in the light of contemporary biblical studies the foundations have shifted or even crumbled away. What would a late twentieth-century doctrine of holiness, for example, based on a late twentieth-century reading of the Bible, look like?

Some of the other groups continue work begun at the last Institute, though with a different slant. The Wesley Studies group is responsible for giving attention to Wesley's understanding of the faith as revealed by what he did, his style of ministry, and the media by which he developed his thought. The group on Methodist Economic and Social Teaching and the Challenge of Liberation Theology focuses on the place of the poor, the group on Evangelism and Doctrine on the varieties of our traditions and on the integration of the personal, social, and political dimensions of the good news of the kingdom. Just as the doctrinal group at the last Institute concentrated on the Lima Statement, *Baptism, Eucharist and Ministry*, so the present group on Contemporary Methodist Theology and Doctrinal Consensus addresses the issues raised by the World Council of Churches' study on the apostolic faith and related papers.[1]

The other new group this time is the one on the Nineteenth Century. As a logical development of our work last time, we were made to see very clearly that Methodist tradition could not be arbitrarily defined as that period in John Wesley's life from around 1720 to some time shortly after 1738. As I have already argued, our traditions are formed for good and ill by all our history and in various ways. The nineteenth century is of course the period concerning which most of us know least about each other. In our geographical separation we went our separate ways, and in our different settings developed differently. If we concentrate exclusively on the Wesley of Oxford and Aldersgate and the field preaching, we allow ourselves to ignore these varied directions and are surprised by the differences we discover when we meet. A closer study of the intervening two centuries and a better sharing of the study will help us all not only to understand one another's peculiarities but also to learn from each other.

This Institute attempts to develop further what we did experimentally last time, that is, interdisciplinary work. In a university setting, of all places, where the ideal is that those who belong to different branches of learning should converse and educate each other, it would be disastrous for the Institute to fragment into six mini-Institutes, each pursuing a separate theme. In any case these different lines of inquiry are touching on common themes, the significance of the poor, for example, and can benefit each other, and we all need to learn what historians are saying about Wesley, or biblical scholars about the Bible, if we are to build on those foundations.

There is provision in the program of the second week for a disputation. Those with memories of earlier Institutes look back on such events as the highlights of the meetings as some issue emerged and was debated, often with considerable vigor. It is not an event which can be manufactured, but which must arise naturally as the work progresses. In such a gathering one cannot expect complete harmony on all points of general interest, but becoming clear about our differences as of value in itself. So much for our program, our theme, and some of its implications.

Perhaps, finally, it would be useful to say something about Oxford. Why the *Oxford* Institute? What significance does our place of meeting have for the work we do? The original vision was that Methodists should work together in the setting which influenced the beginnings of Methodism so much. It has not been possible to keep to all of that original vision. Lincoln College, the college of which John Wesley was a fellow, is too small for the size to which we have grown. The particular colleges in which we now meet have no special significance for Methodism; indeed in Wesley's day they did not exist. Oxford too has changed. The appearance of the town and the style of university life have dramatically altered. That is to be expected as a result of industrialization, on the one hand, and the growth of scientific disciplines in the university, on the other. And of course, though we meet in Oxford with the University all around us, we are not thoroughly immersed in its life and cannot catch its inner spirit.

It is not surprising, therefore, that it is sometimes suggested that we should meet elsewhere, and various advantages for that can be suggested. It is a complicated issue, but I hope a move will be resisted for the following reason, and I mention it because it is part and parcel of the general theme I have been trying to explore: the streams of our Methodist/Wesleyan traditions are varied in their development and have been fed by various tributaries along the way. But they all have their starting point in John and Charles Wesley and the friends they gathered around them. These are the head waters of our common tradition, the beginning we all have in common. For most of us that is a truth enshrined in books. We learn of it from books. We read of it in Wesley's *Journal* and *Sermons* and *Letters*. And we form an impression of its context as best we can. But, as with the study of the Scripture and the Holy Land, places are the interpreters of writings. The sights and sounds of everyday are part of the context in which things are written. For the Wesleys there were many such places, but few were more formative than Epworth and Oxford, London and Bristol, and of those Oxford is perhaps the most extensively preserved. Here you can sit in Lincoln Chapel and St. Mary's. You can see, if not John's actual room at Lincoln, at least one of the rooms he would have known. If you are lucky you may see in the records of that college the entry of his election and resignation as a fellow. It can of course be dismissed as sentimentality; and an uncritical enthusiasm for sacred sites would be sentimentality. But if a

21

stay among the places the Wesleys frequented can help to make them real for us, strips them of the romanticism in which we shroud them, and enlivens our imagination to understand better what they were about, not only will we gain an important dimension to our history and theology, but we may enter a little more deeply into the communion of saints.

Chapter 2

METHODISTS IN SEARCH OF CONSENSUS

Albert C. Outler

Whatever one might wish to make of the symbolic linkages between the Wesleys and Oxford, they can scarcely be stretched to include this particular venue for the first plenary session of this Institute. Here we are, in a lecture hall of the University Museum. Most of us found our way here from Somerville College and St. Hugh's, along the sidewalks of Keble— none of this, however, with any Methodist patina. We are at the scene of the discomfiture of Bishop Samuel Wilberforce by Dr. Thomas Huxley in their famous debate about Darwin and evolution. There is indeed more than a tinge of irony in our being here at all. The sight of dozens of Methodist theologians from the world around, wending their ways through one of the world's notable collections of Mesozoic fossils, recalled for me a striking aphorism by a distinguished paleontologist friend of mine, when we were hashing over the challenging notions of "punctuated evolution." "Don't forget" said he, "that nobody killed the dinosaurs. The atmosphere changed and they died."

But, hallowed in Methodist lore or not, this is a good place to remember the long succession of choke points in world history, of one sort or another, since time immemorial. And this helps us recall that, in the view of increasing numbers of thoughtful people all over the globe, we stand even now at another one of those "punctuations" in human history when our expectations of the human future can no longer be projected by the simple extrapolation of any of our various familiar "pasts," labelled as "our traditions."

It may be that all times are felt as "times between the times." Human life itself is a succession of "spans" in which "heritages" are received (in whole or part), appropriated (less or more), transvalued (for good or ill) and handed onto the oncoming generations (faithfully or not). This is the root-meaning of the term "tradition;" *tradere* can mean "to hand on;" it can also mean "to betray" (as in I Cor. 11:23). Some "epochs" are bridge-like, facilitating the transition from a half-remembered past on toward a half-expected future. Now and again, however, there are these radical discontinuities (call them "crises," "revolutions," "watersheds" as you will), when accustomed cultural "atmospheres" are altered; when no shared past suffices to project the probable future.

The evidence has been accumulating now for some time that ours is such a time of *atmospheric* change, in almost every quarter of the globe. Take, as one example from a dozen, the alterations of our hopes for a bright human future. When I was young, there was a hymn that distilled the optimism of the times, dominated as they were by what looked like a promising "Euro-centered" global culture:

> The day of dawning brotherhood
> Breaks on our eager eyes
> And human hatreds flee before
> The radiant eastern skies.[1]

I can remember how hopeful it all once sounded. Now it sticks in our throats.

The rate of these changes of atmosphere and "consciousness" in human self-awareness seems to have accelerated in the past three decades. The once lush bowers of our "Western" utopianisms (including the Marxist versions, too) seem to be withered and seared. The world I knew in its summertime and autumn has come to have a wintry look; only a few of us are left from then to rake up the fallen leaves from

> . . . those boughs which shake against the
> cold. Bare, ruin'd choirs,
> Where late the sweet birds sang.[2]

We cannot tarry longer to argue all this out or debate what such doomsaying portends. It is enough for our purposes to proffer a tentative thesis that what is now going on is something different from those "paradigm-shifts" that Thomas Kuhn has taught us to recognize in the history of Western scientific revolutions. The Kuhn-type shifts occurred, and still do, within the unfoldings of the processes of a relatively stable "world" of scientific inquiry and technological transformation. What some of us think we see now is more like one of those complex tectonic slippages between the "quarters" of the globe ("Western," "Eastern," "Northern," "Southern").

What our current foreseers are pointing to is what Langdon Gilkey spoke of, some ten years ago, as "the death of the Western deity of progress"[3] and the consequent "grief-work" of the children and grandchildren of the Enlightenment. I grew up with many progressive souls happily enchanted with the human prospect of the "heavenly city" being brought down to earth (i.e., chiefly in Europe and North America; where else?) and there being radically secularized for export to the rest of the world—again, for the benefit of the whole of humanity; what else?[4] Another way of noticing these basic changes in cultural self-understanding is to compare, say, J. B. Bury's famous *Idea of Progress* (1920)[5] and Robert Nisbet's more recent *History of the Idea of Progress* (1980). The contrast is stark, but it reflects much less a body of new data than a profound alteration of perspectives on the "new" human scene.[6]

From the other side, we are aware of the reaction of a "new" and frankly gnostic utopianism-in-renascence, focused in "the human potential movement," ESP, reincarnation, parapsychology, etc. Its emerging canon is previsaged in *Gnosis: A Journal of the Western Inner Traditions* and in the more familiar *New Age Journal*, with its "official" *1988 Guide to New Age Living*. For a thoughtful appraisal of these new developments from the older utopianisms, cf. David Toolan, S.J., *Facing West from California's Shores: A Jesuit's Journey into New Age Consciousness* (New York: Crossroad, 1987).

What is happening, or so it seems to me, is an emergent cultural crisis of global proportions, in deep discontinuity with the patterns of the past five centuries or more, with little or no consensus among observers as to the probable, or even desirable, shape of "the world to come." On the one hand, the epoch of the European dominance of the planet—colonialism, faith in science and technology as panaceas—has lapsed. The notion of idealized humanity as the "essence" of religion (as in Feuerbach, *The Essence of Christianity*, (1841)[7] has lost credibility even among the secular humanists. The "European millennium" (9th to the 19th centuries) is past or passing, with no clear vision yet discernible of what may come hereafter.

On the other hand, the Christian cause has always been at risk insofar as it has ever yoked its fortunes to any given culture at any time, anywhere. Hellenism nearly did it in, followed by Caesaropapism, and after that, feudalism, with its unholy alliances between throne and altar, church and state. The iconoclasts have rarely been helpful, but neither have the "domesticators," who managed to douse the spark in what was meant to be a revolutionary maxim: "The Christians live *in* the world [any world] but are not *of* it [this particular earthbound domain or any other]."[8] There are many tasks for Christians in times of crisis, but one has always been primary: to search out and seek renewal of those priorities in the gospel message that surpass any and all cultural particularities. Thus, in the opening stages of an epoch which does not even have an identifying praenomen as yet ("post-Enlightenment," "post-colonial," "post-modern," or whatever), one of our imperatives is to do what we can to identify the vital residues of perennial Christian teaching, wherever they are to be found,

25

and to reweave these into the fabric of the new future, with all its baffling cultural pluralisms.

One of the obvious "signs" of these "post-everything" times is the rediscovery and acknowledgment of the hidden depths of the human talent for self-stultification and social "deconstruction" (about which the biblical narrative is so graphic, even if there is scarcely anything that pretends to "explain" it all). Some of us may gag at the phrase, "original sin." We may leave Wesley's sermon of that title unread; we may reject its thesis. We may try to "explain" the chilling horrors of "man's inhumanity to man" by appeals to psychological or political casualties. But the harsh realities of the human insufficiency to achieve its own incurved ends (both the well-intentioned ones *and* the malevolent ones), remains.

Despite all our scientific and technological prowess, we now see "the mystery of iniquity" in garish new lights (one needs only to mention AIDS, or "world hunger," or pollution, or The Bomb, or whatever). Wesley abridged the Anglican Article "Of Original or Birth-Sin," but he kept its gist ("the corruption of the nature of every man, whereby [they are] very far gone from original righteousness and of [their] own nature inclined to evil, and that continually").[9] What are Methodists (so many of them Pelagian without overt avowal) going to do about the possible updating of any such stark first premise in Christian anthropology?[10]

Many of us might readily agree that the traditional answers to these ancient perplexities have been too doctrinaire, especially in the West, with its heavy emphasis on sin as guilt and on grace as commutation (as in St. Anselm—and in Protestant scholasticism). But even those of us who (with Wesley) feel more at home with the Eastern traditions—about sin as the tragic spoliation of the divine image—have failed thus far in a credible reformulation of the older traditions of salvation as the restoration of that image by the grace of "participation."[11] Thus, we are equally hard pressed to provide a wholly credible version of authentic *gospel* for the wretched of the earth (the wretched poor, the wretched rich, the wretched powerless and the wretched powerful—the tragic multitude whose hearts are "restless" because they have not found their proper "rest" in God).[12]

From the beginning, Methodist theologies have been taprooted in soteriology and salvation and have struggled heroically with these deeply biblical concerns in whatever their human circumstances. And Methodists who know their origins will know in advance that "ideologies" of any sort (including "orthodoxy") have never been enough—yesterday, today, or whenever. This would remind us that any prospect of being "new creatures in Christ" in a new age (or any age) depends upon something transcultural, the awareness of which Wesley identified, in different *verbal* forms, as the distinctive Christian fundamentals. Take, for example, a late summation:

I mean those [truths] which relate to the eternal Son of God and the Spirit of God—to the Son, giving himself to be a propitiation for the sins of the world; and to the Spirit of God renewing men [and women] in that image of God wherein they were created.[13]

If such language sounds quaint, what we have is a hermeneutical problem. If such basic notions are incredible or incapable of credible reformulation, then a very different question arises—not more "difficult," theoretically, but far more ominous in terms of the Christian faith itself. For the *Christian essentials* are pre-European and non-"Caucasian" and have already had a tortuous history of challenge and response from crisis to crisis, from culture to culture. This, one might have thought, is the point of Galatians 3:22–26 and of the good news that we "are all one in Christ Jesus." But Methodists should take particular notice of Wesley's special accent upon *pneumatology*, as one of the crucial clues to his Christology, which, in turn, is the key to his biblical hermeneutics in general.

Another "sign" of the new times ahead is the growing awareness of the paradox (or is it only an habituated confusion?) of Christian unity-in-diversity and allowable diversity in Christian unity. There was a time, as in the New Testament and early church, when diversity-in-unity could be taken for granted. Yet very soon the questions about diversity had to cope with "heresy": that was the point at which differences (often "non-theological") generated unreconciled division. Presently, however, as the ideal of unity came to be absolutized, this begat dogmatism and mutual rejections as the unnatural consequence. The first stages of *modern* ecumenism included the forevision of a recovered unity as a correlative of our utopian hopes and expectations in other spheres of human interest, as well. We cannot tarry to speak of the altered atmosphere in a post-utopian ecumenism.[14]

It may be enough to note that the ancient bipolarities of the church catholic and the churches local (as the biblical integer of the "Body of Christ") have more lately been distorted by the church curial (dispersed amongst the "denominations"), leaving the cause of Christian unity at the "grass-roots" more hopeful than it is currently anywhere in "the upper circles."

Methodism has had its own history framed by these larger developments and now has its future complicated by them. Wesley and most of the early Methodists took unity-in-diversity for granted; Wesley's notorious disparagements of "orthodoxy" and "opinions" were reckless, partly because he could take the "bottom-line" of classical Christian teaching for granted.[15] It is better balanced to realize that this was his ill-chosen way of rejecting dogmatism as a *method* and of reaffirming the older traditions of "catholic spirit"—which is to say, Christian unity as *koinonia* in Christ, among those already consented in *essential* Christian doctrine.[16] John

27

Wesley cannot be absolved of responsibility in the standard preference among Methodists for emotivist theologies, or for the unrealistic assumptions about our generic identity as a tribe of denominational clans. It is hard to read Wesley's last letter to Methodists in America without a pang:

> ... Time has shaken me by the hand and death is not far behind [as indeed it was, only 30 days later].... See that you never give place to one thought of separating from your brethren in Europe. Lose no opportunity of declaring to all men that the Methodists are one people in all the world, and that it is their full determination so to continue.[17]

It was a noble vision, then and now—but it did not correspond to the facts then or thereafter. But the Methodists were not a "no people," either (as in I Peter 2:10) and still are not. This is why, as dissentient as we are, we have deep feelings of family ties binding us together.

I recall once asking Bishop Paul Ellis how "free" his Free Methodists were. His response was reflex: "At least as free as United Methodists are *united*!" And we both understood our kinship not only in Christ but also in our shared traditions, even as we also recognized the deep anomalies in our respective histories, in which our diversities-in-unity had been tilted in the wrong direction. And we both understood that at the heart of our shared tradition was a trinitarian doctrine of the Holy Spirit that we had learned from Scripture and Wesley and that Wesley had learned from Scripture and early Christian tradition.[18]

There is much else that we can learn from Wesley about the sort of consensus that we shall need in an uncertain future, if we are to continue to fulfill our mission as Methodists—even as we look ahead to the sublation of our denominations into that larger unity that God has willed for us. Moreover, because this mission is rooted in a heritage that reaches back through space and time (a heritage that does not start with the Wesleys), we ought to be able to recognize its relevance in any epoch that may be coming up.

I have already confessed to my suspicions that what some of us in my generation were taught to think of as the Ecumenical Second Coming has now, for the time being, been put "on hold" by the church curial. I share a deep anxiety about the current situation with a wise old Benedictine friend who spoke in a recent private letter of "our bleak ecumenical outlook *ad interim*." This is why I am so concerned, during that interim, about new approaches to the vexed problem of *intercommunion*—no plastering over, ignoring the serious difficulties involved, no cheapening of the grace of Eucharist unity. But the painful business of shared prayer and witness without communion cannot be prolonged forever, and "private eucharistic hospitality" is unacceptable, on principle. We must have carefully safeguarded, "occasional" shared Eucharists, rightly understood as *eschatological signs* of a Christian future yet to come. "Even so, Lord Jesus, come quickly!"

Most of us are already involved, one way or another, in the current renascence of Faith and Order questions in the World Council of Churches and in ecumenical ventures all over the world. There is, for example, nothing new and not much final in the now famous *Baptism, Eucharist, Ministry* document, but the unprecedented interest that it has aroused betokens a new level of consciousness among the people of God. There is "The Lima Liturgy" which has been widely received and experimented with, in many likely places—and a few very "unlikely" places, too. There is a vigorous beginning of a new and mildly audacious quest for consensus as to spirit and content of "The Apostolic Faith" that the Christian motley could confess together. There is even hopeful talk about another World Conference on Faith and Order before the century is out (five years ago, the date was "set"; now it is indefinite).

There is much in all of this ecumenical ferment that is encouraging; and we can take pride in the involvement in the "new ecumenism" of many from our younger generation of Methodist leaders. We should take note of the pre-European orientations of Christianity in its origins, the non-Caucasian components in its early context, its emergence and stabilizations in what has come to be called "the Near East" (actually, the Eastern Mediterranean littoral). Christianity, in its ante-Nicene decades, was the faith of an illicit community widely diverse and unaccountably united (in any of the scenarios of "unity" to which most of us are accustomed). This is not to substitute "history" as a distraction from our exigent current crises; only to suggest added resources for our understanding of the current scene and some options for Christians that seem to have been ignored by current Christian partisans. The early Christians were also scorned by those entrenched in power but they understood Christian "martyrdom" in ways that made more of a difference than some of us may have realized—within the community and in the pre-Constantinian "world."[19]

This suggests a Christian future (which could include a Methodist future, too, linked to "new" patterns of Christian unity, which is to say, the old patterns updated). In any such future, Christian identities and continuities will be rediscovered, historical distortions identified, and the "unpredictable" prepared for. This is why, even as a cradle Methodist, I find the current interest in "The Nicaenum" (which I first learned *about* in seminary) to be a promising rallying point for ecumenical consensus—*if*, that is, the phrase includes the christological bracketings of Nicaea (325 A.D.), Constantinople (381), Jerusalem ("St. Cyril's Creed," ca. 318), Chalcedon (451), and the clarifications of Maximos the Confessor (ca. 662).

In the process, *Nicaenum* needs very much to be conjoined both to *"The Apostolicum,"* and to the *regulae fidei* of the ante-Nicene church. For the taproots of both traditions are deeply biblical, monotheistic, and trinitarian—and in the face of new polytheisms, an integration of all this will become increasingly important, even though it will be difficult.

Moreover—and for Methodists, this may be more relevant than we have recognized—the text of 381 was the first "ecumenical creed" with an explicitly trinitarian pneumatology. In this pre-European tradition, the primacy of Scripture is everywhere acknowledged and nowhere reduced to biblicism.[20] The "orthodoxy" of the old creeds can be queried,[21] but their authority has been ignored only at the expense of dire impoverishment. Such an impoverishment will be no less serious in the coming age than in earlier episodes of emotivism in church history.

Finally, any updating of "the Apostolic Faith" will take us backward to a theological perspective and methodology that antedates Western preoccupations with *"systematic* theology" and what has come to be labelled "scholasticism" (including the tradition in which the Wesleys were trained and against which they revolted). But it also points *forward* to the possibility of a theology that is imbued with the biblical and patristic spirit and thus can survive the bankruptcies of Western dogmatisms and "Enlightenment liberalism," in which "liberalism" has been so comfortably domesticated.

At the heart of all the various *theological* ventures, before "scholasticism" captured the Christian mind in the West, there has been a methodological impulse (in varying measure) to understand human speech about God as chiefly reverential and apophatic: to speak carefully *of* God as if *in God's presence* (*coram Deo*) rather than as object (albeit "the Religious Object" or "Being"); in the Bible and in the patristic church, God was more of a Mystery than a "problem." St. Augustine's *Confessions* is the most familiar example of such a theology (often at levels of very high abstraction!). Here prayer and speculation are mingled in unembarrassed intimacy (*praesentia Dei*) and it is presupposed that God's "presence" is a pneumatic operation ("by the inspiration of thy Holy Spirit"). In the famous Anselmian formula, *fides quaerens intellectum* (faith in search of critical understanding, *intellecta*) the operative term is *faith*, the sort of life-giving faith that is a gift of God's own self, *as Holy Spirit*. Thus, it has always been a mere prejudice to suppose that a pneumato-centric theology needs to be less than trinitarian, once one comes to think of the Christian *mysterion* as focused, Eastern-style, as *presiding* in "sacred things" in the *epiclesis* (the prayer to the Holy Spirit). It is the premise in every *epiclesis* that it is the Holy Spirit, and no priest or liturgy, who actualizes Jesus Christ as really and immediately present, not only in the Eucharist but in human hearts and history.[22] Thus it is that the Spirit is understood as Godself revealing "the deep things of God" and thereby leading the faithful in every age and context into "the mind of Christ" (1 Cor. 2:9–16). This ancient notion of true Christian *spirituality* (as in Romans 8:9–21 and 2 Cor. 3:6–18) was spoken of in various ways by many thoughtful Christians, (in prose and poetry, as in *Veni, Creator Spiritus*) long before it was rhymed in eighteenth century rocking-horse couplets by a populist hymn-writer, echoing in iambics his older brother's sermons on "The Witness of the Spirit":

> Spirit of Faith, come down,
> Reveal the things of God,
> And make to us the Godhead known,
> And witness with the blood.
> 'Tis thine the blood to apply
> And give us eyes to see:
> Who did for *every* sinner die
> Hath surely died for *me*.
>
> No man can truly say
> That Jesus is the Lord,
> Unless thou take the veil away
> And *breathe* the living word.
> Then, only then, we feel
> Our interest in the blood
> And cry with joy unspeakable,
> "Thou art my Lord, my God!"
>
> O that the world might know
> The all-atoning Lamb!
> Spirit of Faith, descend and show
> The virtue of his Name:
> The grace which *all* may find,
> The saving power impart,
> And testify to all mankind,
> And speak in every heart.
>
> Inspire the living faith
> (Which whosoe'er receives,
> The witness in himself he hath
> And consciously believes);
> The faith that conquers all
> And doth the mountains move
> And saves whoe'er on Jesus call,
> And perfects them in love.[23]

Here is a *trinitarian* pneumatology: biblical, patristic, and perennial. And all this is preface to my suggestion that a crucial step toward consensus among Methodists of all sorts would be a re-centering of our theologies of the divine-human interaction (*perichoresis*) in pneumatology. It has been in our tradition to speak of the prevenience of the Holy Spirit's actions, in grace in all of its modalities, and also of the absolute divine initiative in all things, from creation to apocatastasis (Acts 3:21). And if something like this was at the heart of the Wesleys' vision of Christian existence, it is plausible that the heirs to that vision should have something of real importance to share amongst themselves and others—as the ecumenical and interfaith dialogues try to climb out of their present ruts.

Three decades ago, in the course of trying to flesh out my barebones acquaintance with the history of Christian doctrine in terms of its *development*, I began to see a Wesley more interesting and resourceful than his hagiographers had made him out, and someone rather different from the stereotypes in the minds of my fellow-historians with which they have been supplied, largely by the Methodists themselves! I had already "learned" from the stereotypes that Wesley was not a theologians' theologian, that he was not a "complete" or systematic theologian, that he was content to accept and borrow from many traditional statements very much as they stood (as in *A Christian Library* and *The Arminian Magazine*). But even with his eclectic methods and his eristic ways of trying to cope with the barrenness of religious formality and with the irresponsibilities of antinomianism, there was in the Wesleys a fresh focus on *grace* as a pneumatological key to the interpretation of Christian existence. It seemed to me then, and still does, that heirs to this synthesis (not new, but not conventional either) ought to understand, at least as well as any other Christian tribe, the realities of the rule of grace, since they would have been taught from the beginning that it is the Holy Spirit who is "pre-eminently" the Giver of Grace.[24] All of this has made it seem clear to me that in the Wesleys there was an integrated theological agenda that reached back into the fonts of classical Christianity and, therefore, could be made to look forward into a "post-everything" age with a soteriology that is ecumenical enough to be of genuine interest and relevance to men and women who are no longer confident of *self*-salvation.

For they, too, had set out to save their own souls—in dead earnest—and had failed. John's first reported conversion was in 1725, from "levity" to an "entire dedication to God." This gave him a Pelagian syllogism. First premise: an entire devotion of one's life to God is a precondition of salvation. Second premise: I have made such a dedication. Conclusion: I am entitled to the *hope* of God's salvation.[25] A second conversion (1727) was a mystical illumination—not unlike St. Augustine's experience recounted in *Confession* VII (*not* the more climactic one in Book VIII). This preoccupation with self-salvation shows up in his rejection of the Epworth "living" (and with it, his filial duties). It also set him up as an easy target for the challenges of the Moravians (Peter Böhler, et al.). But it also gave him hopeful glimpses of "the promise; but it is afar off."[26]

The conversion ("Aldersgate") of May 24, was a good deal more than an acquiescence in the Moravian arguments, much more than a "strangely warmed heart," (his self-analytic phrase that has become a misleading slogan for Methodists ever since). It was a final and sincere "Yes" to Spangenberg's pointed queries, just mentioned. "Does the Spirit of God *witness with your spirit* that you are a child of God? . . . Do you know Jesus Christ? . . . Do you know that he has saved you?"[27]

"Aldersgate" was Wesley's "experience" of "assurance" (clearly the operation of the Holy Spirit) of pardon and salvation and, since it was so utterly spontaneous, it was his confirmation of the truth of the doctrine of salvation by faith *alone*. It was, for him, a reenactment of Romans 8 (after ten years of Romans 7, and especially of vv. 19–24!). But a strange ambivalence continued as an aftermath for many months. He still spoke of "heaviness."[28] On Sunday, May 28, he "waked in peace but not in joy." That summer, in Marienborn, "when the congregation saw Wesley to be *homo perturbatus* and that his head had gained an ascendancy over his heart, . . . they deemed it not prudent to admit him to the Holy Communion."[29]

"Aldersgate" was *the* decisive moment in John Wesley's career and it is meet and right to celebrate it, even as Methodists have these 250 years, so long as it is clear that its only vicarious effect is insight and inspiration. But better than pilgrimages, and railway engines *in memoriam*, would be for us to read, mark, learn, and inwardly digest his cluster of seven sermons from the formative days of the Revival (Nos. 5–12), and then round them off with the two "discourses" on "The Witness of the Spirit," plus their complement, "The Witness of Our Own Spirit" (foil and counterfoil to the polarities of objectivity and subjectivity in Christian spirituality). Together, this cluster amounts to a neat demonstration of a theology born of the intellectual love of God and a theology *praesentia Dei*.

What is evident in these sermons (though not more so than in other distillations throughout the corpus) is the evangelical core of Wesley's version "the Apostolic Faith": *salvation by grace through faith.*[30] Christian life is "life in Christ," "life in the Spirit": life informed and matured by the Spirit's gifts and fruits. The energy in Christian existence comes from the Spirit's initiative (prevenience is of its essence), in all the modalities of grace, at every stage of the restoration of the ruined image of God—ruined, that is, but not destroyed.

Wesley's talk about such a trajectory of grace is full of the biblical metaphors for the Spirit's immanence and spontaneity: "breath" and "breathing," "wind" and "glowing," "spiration," "inspiration," "respira-

33

tion." These are clues to Wesley's complex epistemological views that we have not taken sufficient pains to analyze or update. He was a "rationalist," but in a special sense; an "empiricist" of sorts, a "romantic" without exuberance and a "common-sense realist" who never read Kant; but *not* (despite many proof-texts to the contrary) a biblical "literalist" and also not properly a "scholastic." To label him "an apophatic theologian" is, I think, correct but not very helpful, in the light of the relegation of that Eastern tradition to the margins in the West, associated with eccentrics like Nicholas of Cusa, or to "mystics" like Malebranche and the Cambridge Platonists.[31] For Wesley, *God-in-se* is unknown and unknowable, incommunicable in demonstrative language. Religious language never succeeds in *defining* the "religious reality."[32] But God is *Self*-communicating—in creation, history, Torah, prophecy, and, above all, in Jesus and the church. Especially in the New Testament, these "disclosures" are identified as operations of the Holy Spirit and almost always with a christocentric focus. Thus, "life in the Spirit" is a richly laden metaphorical phrase about the human potential as designed—and still being designed:

> [In the new birth] the Spirit, or breath of God is immediately inspired, breathed, into the new-born soul; and the same breath which comes from God returns to God. As it is continually received by faith, so it is continued back—by love, by prayer and praise (love, prayer and praise being the breath of every soul which is truly born of God). And by this new kind of *spiritual respiration*, spiritual life is not only sustained but increased, day by day, together with spiritual strength, motion and sensation—all the senses of the soul being now awake and capable of "discerning spiritual good and evil."[33]

Here, then is a spirituality that is unselfconsciously biblical, patristic, and "objective."[34] It is therapeutic in the redeemed and revolutionary in its social implications. Its agenda is the entire consecrations of the whole of life to God (the intellect emphatically included) but less with pious advertisement than in actual ethical transformations. It breathes an Eastern air with its emphases on the divine-human *perichoresis* (interaction), on "participation" and "perfection" as *teleiosis* ("perfecting perfection"). This gives it an odd scent in Western nostrils (sensitive as we have been to clues from courtrooms and codices). But the interesting question here is not which tradition is "better or worse," but whether the perennial truths in each tradition may survive into a post-Western future—and how, even now, they could help rescue Methodism from its current and various domestications.

Christian spirituality has had a tendency, in some cases, to generate more solemnity than real "joy," and in others, to prompt ecstasies that lose touch with reality. . . . Remember Wesley's report, after "Aldersgate":

"I waked in peace but not joy." Once the Revival had begun to flourish, Wesley began to find a vital balance between earnestness and joy, of joy as the aura that goes with absorption in significant function. Thereafter, he finds it easy to speak of "holiness and happiness" in the same breath. There is, indeed, a sort of "ode to joy" in "The Witness of Our Own Spirit," par. 16–17; where "joy" is reckoned specifically as a fruit of the Holy Spirit (Gal. 5:22):

> I rejoice because the sense of God's love to me hath, by the same Spirit, wrought in me to love *him*—and to love, for his sake, every child of man, every soul that he hath made. I rejoice because I both see and feel, through the inspiration of God's Holy Spirit, that all my works are wrought "in him, yea and that it is he who worketh all my works in me. . . ." This is not a "natural joy". . . . Christian joy is in obedience; . . . we rejoice in walking according to "the covenant of grace. . . ."[35]

This way of doing theology is not "systematic" (in the Western sense) but it is not incoherent or obscurantist, either. It has its doctrinal integrity but this functions less as normed (e.g., *Augustana Invariata*!) than norming—and if this seems a mere quibble, we have a serious hermeneutical misunderstanding of the difference between mechanical and organic norms. For Wesley, the theological *crux*, in questions of theological method, lies in the difference between formal constructs of all sorts ("orthodoxy," "orthopraxy," "prophetic passion," ideals—in his day the term "ideology" had not been coined) *and* various evocations of the realities and into the realities and imperatives of the Encompassing Mystery through insights vouchsafed to the eyes and ears of faith, hope, and love by the Holy Spirit—and thereby rendered efficacious (Matt. 7:15–23). There is less "relief" in authentic Christian "assurance" than there are imperatives that are implicit in "the Rule of God." The Christian life is aimed at the complete sacralization of life (what Wesley meant by "holiness of heart and life"). It is the whole "harvest of the Spirit" (Gal. 5:22–23). This is actualized in personal life and society by "faith that is energized by love" (and never mindless love at that).

As Wesley grew old, this vision of sanctification stretched out to wider horizons and became less and less doctrinaire. One can see this especially in a cluster of five sermons from the years of 1788–90.[36]

> True religion is right tempers toward God and man. It is, in two words, gratitude and benevolence. . . . It is the loving God with all our hearts, and our neighbors as ourselves. . . . This begins when we begin to know God by the teaching of his own Spirit. As soon as the Father of spirits reveals the Son in our hearts and the Son reveals the Father, the love of God is shed abroad in our hearts. Then, and not till then, we are [truly] happy. We are happy, first, in the consciousness of God's favor, which indeed is better than life itself; then in all the heavenly

tempers which he hath wrought in us [in our creation as persons] by his Spirit; again, in the testimony of his Spirit, that all our [good] works please him; and lastly, in the testimony of our own spirits, that "in simplicity and godly sincerity, we have had our conversation [life-styles] in the world." Standing fast in this liberty from sin and sorrow, wherewith Christ hath made them free, real Christians "rejoice evermore, pray without ceasing, and in everything give thanks." And their happiness still increases as they grow up into the measure of the stature of the fullness of Christ."[37]

Such a way of theologizing—in the presence of God and the People of God—is, admittedly, homiletical, nonanalytical, not without an abundant share of inconsistencies and fixed ideas. Its value increases, however, as it is mingled with the whole range of Christian fundamentals as they have been pondered and developed in and through the crises that have threatened the identity and continuity of the gospel across the centuries. But it is this evidence of Wesley's "at-homeness" in the Christian tradition as a whole (in Scripture and the church) that suggests a durable *consensus fidelium* that can surpass cultural contexts and that can undergird the church ecumenical, in an altered future. It saved him from biblic*ism*, traditional*ism*, rational*ism*, and narcis*sism*. It could provide contemporary Methodism a way of escape from cultural relativism, triumphalism, and the confusions of contemporaneity (confusions that have become chronic in a process of accelerating change).

We can learn much about our Methodist theological heritage in Britain and North America from Thomas Langford's helpful source-books, *Practical Divinity: Theology in the Wesleyan Tradition* (1983) and *Wesleyan Theology* (1984). But we need to learn much more about the Methodist traditions on the European Continent, in Africa, Asia (especially in Malaysia, Singapore, and now South Korea), in Australasia and Latin America, and the residual influences of Methodism in the "united churches" in which Methodists have cast their lot (as in Canada and India). We need to learn, non-defensively, how modest the expectations are from non-Methodist quarters as to what "World Methodism" may have to bring, by way of doctrinal treasures, into the shared offertory of the Great Ecumenical Eucharist. We have nothing to compare with the *Augustana*, with Calvin's *Institutes*, or the *Westminster Shorter Catechism*. We do not even have an anomaly like *The Confession of Dositheus* (in Orthodoxy). Indeed, in the Methodist denominations with origins in *The Methodist Episcopal Church* of 1784 and 1808, we have no official creeds, since Wesley, in his hasty abridgments (1784) of the Thirty-nine Articles, simply struck out Article VIII *in toto* and nobody in "The Christmas Conference," or thereafter, has thought to put it back!

Even so — and despite our other de-traditionings over two centuries— there is still a legacy of doxological theology in Methodism (as Geoffrey Wainwright has sought to remind us in his notable volume, *Doxology*, 1980). Traditional Methodist theology has been less liturgical than pneumatological, more akin to evangelical catholicism (sacramental but not sacerdotal) than to evangelical Protestantism (on points like *sola Scriptura*, predestination, single justification, and "holiness"). We ought to have been less easily domesticated and denominationalized, *in principle*, than we have been in sad fact. And insofar as our heritage is alive, it makes for a still promising linkage between the pre-European Christianity that Wesley regarded as paradigmatic *and* the Evangelical Revival and its "enthusiasms" (in which he flourished),[38] *and* the "post-whatever" epoch that looms so vaguely before us. Most Methodists whom I know are in heart-to-heart engagement with the daily turmoils of their current crises, as indeed they ought to be, with as much wisdom as they can muster and as little self-righteousness as their partisan zeals will allow. But we must also be engaged in reclaiming our heritage, which reaches not only to the Wesleys, but far behind them, to older Christian wisdoms still viable. And this means a *new* (old?) view of "Tradition and traditions"—wherein "Tradition" is understood as God's *actus tradendi* of the Logos, and where "*t*radition" is recognized as the perduring identity and continuity of what was begun at Pentecost (constitutive and bound at the least to what Wesley reduced to "the Scriptures and the Primitive Church").[39] This would give us more clarity in distinguishing "Tradition" from "tradition*s*," which chiefly denotes those ecclesiastical mores and customs of whose variety there shall be no end.

At the heart of our Wesleyan legacy is an ample vision of grace—the grace of our Lord Jesus Christ which is the love of God manifest in the *koinonia* of the Holy Spirit—and this has given us the core of whatever consensus we have ever had or can hope for in the times ahead. Any such consensus must allow for variety in formulation; it must require an unfeigned acknowledgment of its imperatives to holiness—the love of God and neighbor. The need for grace is radical, the offer of grace is real, the gift of grace is consummate in Jesus Christ, the Giver of grace is the Holy Spirit (Lord and Life-Giver!). The community of grace is our shared *koinonia* in the Body of Christ joined to the Head and to itself through its "members." The reception of free grace is by true repentance and faith, the rule of grace is the Rule of God, the sign of grace is grateful, self-giving love, the tasks of grace are defined by human wretchedness and need, the confidence of grace is that nothing in all creation can separate us from the love of God in Christ Jesus, our Lord. What of this (other than its verbal dress) would Methodists have to reject, *de fide*? What needs to be added or altered, save by implication or emphasis? Could we, then, take a focus on grace as the nucleating notion of a Methodist consensus?

In such times there is bound to be an honest question about Methodism's future. Do we still agree with the early Methodists that we "were raised up," *ad hoc* and *ad interim*, "to reform the nation[s], especially the church[es]," and to spread "scriptural holiness over the lands?" And if these tasks are still unfinished, what are our continued reasons for being? Are we not still committed to those primal Kingdom-tasks: to be more truly effectual instruments of God's peace and righteousness—peace and righteousness in the churches and the world? But would we or would we not be more faithful to God's design for us if we were willing to lose our denominational lives if that would hasten the *communio in sacris* that Jesus prayed for and that the Father wills—a unity-in-sacred-things that cherishes all the diversities that enhance *community* and that allows all other concerns to ease off, or slip away? Otherwise, have any of our denominations a first or even a second lien on any future worthy of the Christian name?

The Wesleys framed the Christian future within the original metaphors of liberation and pilgrimage, from the Exodus and the sojourn in Sinai. In 1762, Charles turned this eschatological vision into a hymn for Christian pilgrims in his day, and any other. It is a hymn that has been better known and loved better in other parts of Methodism than in America; The United Methodist Church has discarded it from its next new *Hymnal*. But one of the truly great moments of my life, among many, was joining in its full-throated affirmation as the closing hymn at the "Re-opening of Wesley's Chapel" on All Saints Day, 1978. I hope, therefore, that its message is never lost among us—and certainly not its vivid understanding of the trinitarian base of our upholding faith in the gracious *Providence* of the Triune God. We shall, I think, need such a faith more in the years ahead than we can know now:

> Captain of Israel's host, and guide
> Of all who seek the land above,
> Beneath thy shadow we abide,
> The cloud of thy protecting love.

> Our strength, thy grace; our rule, thy Word
> Our end: the glory of the Lord.
> By thine unerring Spirit led,
> We shall not in the desert stray;
> We shall not full direction need [lack]
> Or miss our providential way.
> As far from danger as from fear,
> While love, Almighty Love, is near.

> Amen.

Chapter 3

RIGHTEOUSNESS AND JUSTIFICATION

C. K. Barrett

The subject before us is not one of my own choosing, though it meets my warm approval. It was suggested to me as one on which a student of the Bible might be able to make a contribution to the total Methodist theological enterprise, might give rise to profitable reflection on a number of practical topics, and might thus vindicate the claims of serious biblical study to be able to address the modern world in coherent, intelligible, critical, and creative terms. There are perhaps not very many new things to say about justification, but the old things that have many times been said are more worth hearing than some of the latest novelties.

More important in this context than my approval is the fact that the subject would have been welcomed by John Wesley. You will recall the beginning of his sermon on justification by faith.

> How a sinner may be justified before God, the Lord and Judge of all, is a question of no common importance to every child of man. It contains the foundation of all our hope, inasmuch as while we are at enmity with God there can be no true peace, no solid joy, either in time or in eternity.[1]

The first question addressed by the first Methodist Conference, in 1744, was, What to teach; and under this heading the first matter settled was the meaning of justification. We shall return to the Conference's substantially correct definition in due course; for the present, however, it is enough to note what was the beginning of their dogmatics.

It may of course be remarked that in their attitude Wesley and his preachers were merely following what was still dogmatic convention in the eighteenth century. Wesley professed great respect for the Homilies of the Church of England (and some of his followers might study them still to their advantage). In the first Church of England *Book of Homilies*,[2] the first part of the Sermon on the Salvation of Mankind begins with a clearer and fuller statement than the opening paragraph of Wesley's sermon.

> Because all men be sinners and offenders against God, and breakers of his law and commandments, therefore can no man by his own acts, works, and deeds, seem they ever so good, be justified and made righteous before God; but every man of necessity is constrained to seek for another righteousness or justification, to be received at God's own hands, that is to say, the remission, pardon, and forgiveness of his sins and trespasses in such things as he hath offended. And this justification or righteousness, which we so receive by God's mercy and Christ's merits, embraced by faith, is taken, accepted, and allowed of God for our perfect and full justification.

The Homilies reflect in turn the strong Lutheran element in early Anglicanism, though justification is a matter on which we do not need to distinguish too nicely between Wittenberg and Geneva; that this stream tended to run dry in the Caroline Divines and the Cambridge Platonists did not greatly affect its official standing in Wesley's time, though how far it was personally apprehended is another matter. If it did no more, it served as a cardinal piece of anti-Roman propaganda.

But was John Wesley right to lay so much stress on justification? Was Charles Wesley right when he referred to it as the foundation on which our church was built? That the great exponent of justification in the New Testament is Paul goes without saying; but does it play a central part even in Paul's thought? Or is it a passing feature of a controversy between Paul and Jews (or Jewish Christians) which both flared and faded in the first century?

The centrality of justification in Paul's thought has been denied by some of the greatest New Testament scholars of our time. One of Albert Schweitzer's most famous sentences is:

> The doctrine of righteousness by faith is therefore a subsidiary crater, which has formed within the rim of the main crater—the mystical doctrine of redemption through the being-in-Christ.[3]

It is impossible here to trace the complicated argument by which Schweitzer reaches this conclusion, but it is worthwhile to note two things which will return in the course of our discussion. One is that Schweitzer finds the roots of Paul's notion of a mystical being in Christ in that primitive eschatological worldview which he traces back to Jesus himself, and that this notion of righteousness is linked with a view of faith that rejects not only works done in obedience to Jewish law, but works in general. "He thus closes the pathway to a theory of ethics."[4]

W. Wrede, with whom in other matters Schweitzer could disagree sharply enough, writes in a similar vein:

> The best known of Paul's ideas, the so-called doctrine of justification by faith, has not yet been mentioned. Our silence in itself implies a judgment. The

40

Reformation has accustomed us to look upon this as the central point of Pauline doctrine; but it is not so. In fact the whole Pauline religion can be expounded without a word being said about this doctrine, unless it be in the part devoted to the law.[5]

Justification is a *Kampfeslehre* and belongs with the rejection of Judaism; and it is a doctrine that must give rise to problems in the realm of ethics. Paul proclaims, "Christ is the end of the law" (Rom. 10:4), and when he does so he refers to the whole law:

Why are not the moral commands excepted? How can belief in Christ be opposed to them? Certainly Paul never dreams that the *content* of the moral precepts, such as, the commandments, is false. But he denies the right of the Law to *demand* their fulfillment; he declares that every "thou shalt" is done away. Even this is enigmatic enough.[6]

So far we may seem to have been dealing with ancient history in the interpretation of the New Testament, though the points Schweitzer and Wrede make have not been forgotten. Paul's doctrine was (a) the fruit of a controversy with which we are no longer concerned, and (b) impossible to reconcile with the ethical implications of the Gospel—indeed with Paul's own affirmation that even the justified must stand trial before God at the last judgment. More recent, however, and on different lines, is the work of Krister Stendahl, which was taken up in a fierce refutation by Ernst Käsemann, to which in turn Stendahl replied. I have to admit that I do not find it easy to understand exactly what these two are saying to each other. Stendahl thinks that Käsemann did not understand him correctly; I am not sure, however, that Stendahl understands Käsemann's criticism. Certainly, Stendahl does not seem to me to mean that Paul did not teach the doctrine of justification or that he taught it but considered it trivial and expendable. His title is "Paul and the Introspective Conscience of the West,"[7] and I take it that in this title he claims that Paul has been misunderstood because many generations have read him through the eyes of men like Augustine and Luther, for whom their starting point was provided by the desperate search, *Wie krieg ich einen gnädigen Gott?* or, as Johann von Paltz, anticipating Luther and showing that in this Luther was a representative Westerner, put it, *Quomodo inveniam deum placatum?* According to Stendahl, it is we Western human beings who conduct this search, who are concerned to look into our conscience and find it ill, it is we who know therefore that we must somehow get the forgiveness of our sins.

Not so Paul; and when Paul does develop the doctrine of justification it is not for its own sake, nor in order to have ammunition to fire at the Jews, but in order to establish his mission to the Gentiles and to vindicate their place among the people of God. It follows (according to Stendahl) that the chapters about *Heilsgeschichte*, Romans 9–11, are both the basic source of the doctrine and the core of the epistle, not an appendage to it. Now it is true that, though neither δίκαιος nor δικαιοῦν occurs in Romans 9–11, δικαιοσύνη does occur ten times in a very important passage (9:30–10:6) in which Paul cites the religious history of Jews and Gentiles. It is also true that Augustine and Luther were of different national stock and lived in different ages from Paul's. But did not Paul share an introspective conscience with them? Is even Luther's desire for a God who would be gracious to his sin more poignant than "I do not do the good I want, but the evil I do not want is what I do" (Rom. 7:19)?

There is a distinction here which lies in an important point just under the surface. Paul did have a sensitive introspective conscience, but he got it with the gospel. It was as a Christian that he began to examine himself and to recognize that a good conscience would not justify him (1 Cor. 4:4). He did not become a Christian because he examined himself and his conscience, found the result unsatisfactory, and decided that something had to be done about it. Augustine, and to a greater extent Luther, started at a different point, created by a Christian upbringing; between them and Paul there was a difference but it is not the difference described by Stendahl. Justification and the introspective conscience belong together, but they will not always be related to each other in the same way.

I draw attention here to the fact, but do not develop it, that what I have just said about the conscience is related to the question of Paul's understanding of Torah, and the relation of his understanding to that most widely current in his day. There is a question here which it would take a long time to pursue; I need not say that I have in mind the work of E. P. Sanders and the discussions that have arisen out of it. I shall content myself with the observation, which I think few would dispute, that like his treatment of conscience Paul's treatment of Torah is a Christian product. "For no human being will be justified in his sight by works of the law . . ." (Rom. 3:20; cf. Gal. 2:16) is a Christian judgment, as the misquotation of Ps. 143:2 suggests.

The question is not how frequently Paul refers to justification but the contexts in which he speaks of it, and above all what he says about it. There is of course no doubt that the main source is Romans. If I ask, why did Paul write Romans? we shall be in some danger of never reaching the main theme, for this question is one that has attracted a good deal of recent discussion. But most of the answers to this disputed question are at one in the belief, or implication, that Paul, in this letter to a church he did not personally know, was summing up his understanding of the Christian faith. It matters little whether we describe the letter as Paul's testament or think of it as his introduction of himself to Rome, designed to win a base for his

42

mission to Spain in the far West; in either case he was setting out his understanding of the gospel, and in this the themes of righteousness and justification play a major part. The second source for his teaching on these themes is Galatians, and here too, though in a way more narrowly attached to specific circumstances (for Galatia he did know—too closely perhaps for comfort), Paul sets out the essence of his theology. Those who were making trouble were preaching what they presented as εὐαγγέλιον (1:6–9); it is no such thing, says Paul, and, he implies, I will tell you what the real gospel is. Here indeed we see the doctrine of justification as a *Kampfeslehre*; this in no way diminishes its importance, for the *Kampf* was for the integrity of Christian belief and the existence of the church. There is more in Philippians; there is little in the letters to the Corinthians and Thessalonians, partly or perhaps mainly, because in these letters Paul was concerned with other matters which did not involve doctrinal discussion of this topic (though there are a few verses of great importance in 1 and 2 Corinthians). Paul found it difficult to discuss the roots of Christian faith and life without righteousness and justification.

This is more than enough of what is hardly more than introductory matter. Whether the doctrine is regarded as central or peripheral in Paul's thought—and I have no doubt of its centrality—we are committed to a discussion of it. And the discussion is not easy.

The question is a linguistic one, in more senses than one. Everyone is familiar with Luther's discovery of the meaning of righteousness, which lay at the root of his teaching about justification. He read in the Psalms (31:1b), *In iustitia tua libera me.* But how could God, the judge of all the earth, who must do right, set free one who was undoubtedly guilty? Was it not precisely his *iustitia* that must compel him to incarcerate the guilty, and that in the flames of hell? How could the manifestation of righteousness be a gospel? Yet Paul had written that in the gospel, and constituting it as gospel, as good news, δικαιοσύνη θεοῦ ἀποκαλύπτεται. But behind Latin *iustitia* and Greek δικαιοσύνη was Hebrew צֶדֶק, צְדָקָה; and, more importantly, a wealth of biblical usage waiting to be explored. The linguistic exploration goes on, from Luther to Ziesler, and there will be more of it in the present lecture, though of course I shall assume a great deal. There are, as I have said, other senses in which the question before us may be described as linguistic. The recent ARCIC document on justification comes, more or less, to the conclusion that the disputes of the sixteenth century can be happily left behind because they involved little more than disagreement, unnoticed disagreement, in the use of words. Catholic and Protestant in fact meant very much the same but their use of language was different, and they therefore received the impression that they meant different things. I should be glad, but somewhat surprised, to find myself persuaded that this

43

is not too easy a dodging of difficulties. Were our ancestors really such misguided bigots as to slaughter one another over divergent semantics? Or were they moved by serious, radical theological differences, which might justify, not indeed slaughter, but perhaps ecclesiastical separation? The real semantic problem exists, in fact, in and for both camps, for it consists in the way in which words of fundamental importance slither from one sense to another. It is impossible to attach the same meaning to the word δικαιοσύνη in every passage in which Paul uses the word. In yet another sense (but a related one) the question before us may be said to be a linguistic one, for it raises the problem of myth and of appropriate religious language; but we have far to go before we reach that point.

It is clear that to continue will involve the use of the biblical languages. I shall keep this to a minimum, but I shall not apologize for the method.

So we begin with a question that may at first seem secondary. How should one translate the Hebrew word רָשָׁע? Here I must forbear to provide at once an English translation, since translation is precisely the issue. The word was already giving trouble in antiquity. The Septuagint used a variety of Greek words in their attempt to find a satisfactory rendering; there are at least four that must be noticed: ἄδικος, ἁρματωλός, ἄνομος, and ἀσεβής. Two of these correspond reasonably well with the basic meaning of the Hebrew word, which signifies guilt; it denotes the party found guilty in court; this is precisely the meaning of ἄδικος, the person against whom judgment is given; we may call him or her ἄνομος when a law or legal system is involved. The guilty party is found to be in contravention of the νόμος, the legal basis on which the court is established, the law which the court is commissioned to uphold. Of the other two words, the former, ἁμαρτωλός, represents a moralizing tendency: the guilty person is not found guilty on a mere technicality; morally wrong, he or she has failed to do what he or she is under moral obligation to do. The latter, ἀσεβής, may be described as pietizing: the ἀσεβής is a person who does not σέβεσθαι, worship, as he or she ought; such a person is wrong in religion. It would be easy to describe ἁρματωλός and ἀσεβής as mistranslations, or at least as misleading translations; this in principle they are not, though sometimes they fail to represent the sense of the original correctly. They are (sometimes at least) legitimate semantic developments. There has hardly ever been a court of law that did not claim that its verdicts were related more or less directly to moral judgments. Even hypocritically immoral courts have usually been careful to make the claim, however false it may have been. Thus there is an implication that the ἄδικος is ἁρματωλός: having done what he or she ought not—morally—to have done, or failing to do what he or she ought—morally—to have done. It is not every system of law that had or has a religious element, but the Old

Testament law certainly had one. The person who offends against the law has offended against the lawgiver; the lawgiver is God and one has therefore failed to give God God's due. Such a one is ἀσεβής, an impious, godless person. These semantic developments are to some extent fairly obvious, but it will be important to keep them in mind; to allow for them sufficiently but not too much.

Thus at Exodus 9:27 we meet both רשע and its opposite (denoting the party that wins its case in court), when, after the plague of hail, Pharaoh declares, the Lord is הצדיק, I and my people are הרשעים. Notice the articles: God is the winner, we Egyptians are the losers. But the Greek words are respectively δίκαιος and ἀσεβής. Here God is one of two legal, forensic contestants; in such circumstances God is sure to win (after all, God is also judge; but cf. Ps. 51). When God operates simply as judge, God can be depended upon to make the proper distinction between צדיק and רשע. This comes out with great clarity in the familiar story of Genesis 18, when God threatens to destroy the wicked city, Abraham intercedes for it. God is proposing the wholesale indiscriminate destruction of the entire city. But the population may not be uniform. Perhaps there will be found fifty, forty–five, forty, thirty, twenty, ten innocent people in the city. It would be inconsistent with God's character as judge of the whole earth if these were wiped out along with the guilty. What must not happen is והיה כצדיק כרשע (18:25). A just court will always distinguish between the two; God will always distinguish between the two. It does not seem to occur to Abraham that he is asking God, and God is agreeing, to do precisely what God ought (on Abraham's own argument) not to do. Abraham objects to the treatment of ten innocent people as if they were guilty; he does not seem to mind if 10,000 guilty people are treated as if they were innocent. This is of course a significant inconsistency; considerations not only of evenhanded moral justice but of mercy cannot be kept out of the proceedings when God and a representative of God are involved.

Considerations of mercy, however, do not always appear. They are not in evidence in those famous passages in Isaiah and the Psalms where God's righteousness becomes tantamount to his acts of deliverance. When for example in Isa. 46:13 God declares, "I have brought near my righteousness (צדקתי, τὴν δικαιοσύνην μου, iustitiam meam), it shall not delay, and my salvation shall not tarry" (my translation), God is acting in justice as the judge of all the earth. When Israel was a relatively sinful nation God punished it; now that Israel is at least relatively righteous (in comparison with the Babylonians), God will restore it. This amounts to deliverance, salvation, but this is a secondary consequence. It is unfortunate that the New English Bible and other modern translations in passages such as this translate צדקה by *deliverance*, or some such word; this obscures the very important truth that in delivering God's people God is acting as a righteous judge. The word חסד, usually understood to refer to God's faithful covenant-keeping love, occurs only four times in Deutero-Isaiah. Isa. 40:6 (כל–חסדו כציץ) is clearly irrelevant and only 54:8,10; 55:3 remain. These indeed are important enough, but it is also important to note the contexts in which they are set. 54:8 begins with the outpouring of God's wrath, which Israel undoubtedly deserved; it is when Israel repents and returns that the faithful mercies of David apply. The essential character of God in Deutero-Isaiah is righteousness; it is this that gives the prophet hope.

We have moved along the negative linguistic line, looking primarily at the role of the רשע, the guilty. This was partly to add a little interest to the linguistic investigation but mainly in order that we might meet the words righteousness (δικαιοσύνη) and justify (δικαιοῦν) in their proper forensic setting and hear the Old Testament at precisely the point at which Paul contradicts, or appears to contradict, it. At Exodus 23:7 God expressly declares לא–אצדיק רשע, which interestingly enough the Septuagint turns into a command: οὐ δικαιώσεις τὸν ἀσεβῆ (adding ἕνεκεν δώρων. Isa. 5:23 and Proverbs 24:24 are similar, and Proverbs 17:15 is particularly significant: מצדיק רשע ומרשיע צדיק תועבת יהוה שניהם. Whenever there is a legal dispute one will turn out to be just, the other guilty; you must not justify the guilty or condemn the just. In Exod. 23.7; Isa. 5.23; Prov. 24.24 the unjustifiable person is the ἀσεβής; in Prov. 17.15 he or she is the ἄδικος. It is only against this background that one can understand the force of Paul's assertion that God will do what no just judge will do: he will justify the unjustifiable, the ἀσεβής (Rom. 4:5).

That Paul was aware of the problem thus created appears very clearly in what is perhaps his most explicit and most important treatment of the theme of justification. It focuses somewhat more closely on righteousness (δικαιοσύνη) than on justification (δικαιοῦν), so as to indicate the ambiguity that is always found in this word. When he speaks of the righteousness of God, does he mean God's own righteousness in which God does always what is right, or a righteousness that God graciously confers on human beings, by which sinful human beings may have fellowship with the holy and righteous God? The problem of ambiguity is to a great extent dealt with when we remember the forensic setting to which the vocabulary of righteousness belongs. We may note in passing that no other proposed setting is able so successfully to deal with the ambiguity and with the problem with which we are concerned. There is a righteousness of the judge and a righteousness of the defendant. The same word is appropriately used of both, and though distinct they are related to each other; what matters is the satisfaction of the court, and this cannot be achieved unless (by whatever means) both judge and defendant are δίκαιος. In Rom. 3:21–31 (cf. 1:16,17) Paul finds the root of the gospel in a manifestation of God's righteousness (the fact that so puzzled and distressed Luther). But God had to manifest his righteousness and uphold it precisely because it was liable to be impugned. Shall not the judge of all the earth do right? Abraham asked. But there was no sign that he was doing any such thing—a fact neatly illustrated by Genesis 18. From the Garden of Eden onwards people had been sinning and getting away with it. God had declared (Gen. 2:17), "for in the day that you eat of it you shall die." But Adam had lived to the good old age of 930. God had been passing over (the word is πάρεσις) human beings' sins, neither punishing them as they deserved nor granting them full remission and release (ἄφεσις). The observer might easily draw the conclusion: God does not care; God does not distinguish between right and wrong; the judge is not acting as the judge of all the earth should do; God is not δίκαιος.

This was not all. The human race was not righteous. Paul states the matter baldly in the language of the Old Testament at Rom. 3.10: there is not even one righteous human being. If then the judge wakes up and begins to act as a good judge should, that will mean the end of humanity; and that will mean that God's objective in creation, of a family of human beings living in relation with Godself, has failed. God then must act (and here Ernst Käsemann and Peter Stuhlmacher have a contribution to make) in faithfulness to God's role as creator (as well as judge); God must find a way of justifying the unjustifiable, the ἄδικος, ἁμαρτωλόσς, ἄνομος, ἀσεβής. All this is to be found in Rom. 3:25,26.

But how is God to do it? Are we not going to be pushed into the problem that John Wesley was clearly aware of, the danger of turning justification into a fiction, in which God pretends that black is white? If this happens there is a lie at the heart of the Christian doctrine of salvation.

The key to the problem lies in the essentially forensic character of the whole vocabulary of justification—δικαιοῦν, δικαιοσύνη, and the other words. The matter has never been better stated than by Bultmann, whom I will quote before going on to develop the matter.

> When it connotes the condition for (or essence of) salvation, δικαιοσύνη is a forensic term. It does not mean the ethical quality of a person. It does not mean any quality at all, but a relationship. That is, δικαιοσύνη is not something a person has as his own; rather it is something he has in the verdict of the "forum" . . . to which he is accountable. He has it in the opinion adjudicated to him by another. A man has "righteousness," or is "righteous," when he is acknowledged to be such, and that means, in case such acknowledgment of him is in dispute: when he is "right-wised," "pronounced righteous". . . .[8]

Justification is thus a pre-moral issue; it turns not upon an estimate of moral worth but upon the creation of a relation. This appears clearly in the close parallel between justification and reconciliation, and this is stated unmistakably in Rom. 5:9,10. In each of these verses there are three points; in v. 9, the death of Jesus (expressed in the reference to his blood), justification, and future salvation; in v. 10, the death of Jesus, reconciliation, and future salvation.

There is no essential difference between justification and reconciliation, as John Wesley recognized when he said, "The plain scriptural notion of justification is pardon, the forgiveness of sins." We may recall the sermon,[9] quoted above, and the conclusion of the 1744 Conference: "To be justified is to be pardoned."[10] What Wesley missed is the distinctive representation of pardon, or reconciliation, in the forensic language of righteousness and justification. Reconciliation means the creation of a right relation between two conflicting parties; where there had been enmity and strife, peace prevails. Justification places the contention in a court of law, where the strife is between the judge (who will certainly do right) and the prisoner (who has certainly done wrong). In this strife there is no question on which side right lies. The law is there to accuse, the witnesses are there to prove. The judge will not say (for it would be a lie), You are after all a good person—even a potentially good person. By a creative moral act the judge brings about a good relation in place of the bad one.

We may pursue the parallel theme of reconciliation and that of the creative moral act as we consider one more passage, 2 Cor. 5:20b–21. There is reconciliation in the immediate context. God has committed to us the message of reconciliation. "We beseech you in behalf of Christ, be reconciled to God." Then follows: "For our sake he made him to be sin who knew no sin, so that in him we might become the righteousness of God."

Here are two balanced clauses in which it is claimed first that the sinless Jesus came to occupy that relation of alienation from God most comprehensively defined by the term ἁμαρτία in order that we in him might come to occupy that positive relation with God defined by the term δικαιοσύνη. It is clear now that the focus of the creative moral act is to be found in Christ, and especially in Christ crucified, and we are sent back to the *locus classicus* in Romans 3. It was in Christ that God's righteousness was manifested, and that regardless whether δικαιοσύνη θεοῦ means the righteousness God has in Godself, God's outgoing saving righteousness, or the righteousness that God confers upon the believer. He was set forth by God in a bloody sacrificial death which can be described by the word ἱλαστήριον, which points to, takes up, and transcends the proceedings of the Old Testament Day of Atonement.

48

At this point, I suspect, Wesley would have been content to stop. Yet it is hardly open to us to do so. If we say either that the death of Christ was an atoning sacrifice, or that he has taken (and suffered for) our sins that we may receive his righteousness, we are using the language of myth, and (though we may in the end decide that the truth cannot be fully expressed without the use of myth) we cannot be content to leave it at that without further consideration. There are two ways in which we may turn; and I believe it to be correct to use both.

One is to say that this myth has in fact been historicized. It is additionally worthwhile to note this because it will show that justification is not a mere Pauline eccentricity. In different ways those great but different New Testament scholars J. Jeremias and E. Käsemann have pointed out that the theme of justification is to be found in the Gospels. It is found in the picture of Jesus as the friend of publicans and sinners. This not only represents him as loving and caring for unlovable people who in themselves have nothing to commend them; he is actually creating a relation where none existed. As he eats with his disreputable guests (or hosts), the lost sheep is found, the lost coin is discovered, and the lost son comes home—to God (Luke 15). More explicitly, he forgives sins (Mark 2:5), thus creating a relation where the law had failed to preserve or make one. The same can be seen, in outline, in Jeremias. We may go further and note that by doing all this Jesus became, in the eyes of the law, sin. It would be absurd to claim that the food laws were rigidly observed every time Jesus ate with sinners; in any case, the Gospels explicitly record that the mealtime habits of his associates were matter of complaint (e.g. Mark 7:2). And on their own terms the scribes were right to accuse Jesus of blasphemy, when he claimed to forgive sins. Again, we may turn to the Beatitudes, in which Jesus declares, "Blessed are you poor," which Matthew turns into, "Blessed are the poor in spirit," trying, rather obscurely perhaps, to make it clear that poverty is not simply lack of cash. The poor are pronounced blessed not because it is a good thing to be penniless but because to those who have nothing—and nothing that can get in the way—God gives everything, God's Kingdom. Unlike the rich, who are tempted to think that they can buy anything, the poor can receive the Kingdom in the only way it can be received—as a gift. What thus happened over a brief period and a limited area in history was universalized and made eternal by the event of crucifixion and resurrection.

The other way of dealing with the myth is to see in it the representation of the true being of the human being as God's creation. It is the natural inclination of human beings to establish their own righteousness before God. Paul recognizes this as a feature of his own life before his encounter with Christ (Phil. 3:4–6,9); he had indeed a righteousness of his own, generated by his obedience to law. What he saw in the story of his own life he saw also on a wider scale in the story of his people (Rom. 9:30–10:4). No fault could be found in their religious enthusiasm; they had a zeal for God but it was an uninformed zeal—οὐ κατ᾽ ἐπίγνωσιν; they had got it wrong precisely in that they were seeking to establish their own righteousness, τὴν ἰδίαν δικαιοσύνεν; as long as they were doing this they could not submit to the righteousness of God. In other words, in the courtroom scene they were dispossessing God of God's role as judge of all the earth: righteousness was to be not God's verdict but theirs. To this end they used, or abused, the law that God had given them, a process to which Christ has now put an end by doing what the law could not do (Rom. 8:3) and conferring righteousness on the believer (Rom. 10:2–4).

At this point we may briefly state two familiar inferences of primary importance: justification is of God's grace, and by faith—*sola* gratia and *sola* fide. It is sola gratia because it arises in a situation in which human beings can effectively do nothing and have no claim upon God. We may rebel; we may do nothing; we may seek to establish our own righteousness: none of these courses is effective, and unless God takes the initiative nothing will happen. And when God in grace does this, that is, creating righteousness as a relation, there is nothing we can do but accept or reject that which God has put in hand; and accepting it is faith. There is no question of deserving what comes as a free gift and comes into being in the creative mind of God.

It is for this reason that justification is *articulus stantis vel cadentis ecclesiae*. It means that God is prepared to begin with us as we are; otherwise, even for God, there would be no beginning at all. Justification— and Wesley always emphasized this—is not the whole story, but it is the first chapter without which there would be no story at all. It is best looked at as the eschatological event that it immediately appears to be as soon as it is recalled that it implies God's judgment on human beings. If we think of this in simple futuristic terms we know that after the judgment there comes, for those approved by the Judge, the holiness and bliss of heaven. If the last judgment is anticipated in the verdict of acquittal that justification means, this will be followed by an anticipation of the holiness and bliss of heaven. This is pretty much what Wesley understood by sanctification. The point, however, at which Wesley's understanding of justification is seriously deficient comes into sight here. Justification is indeed the beginning of the Christian life, but it is not a beginning that can be experienced and left behind. Luther was wiser and knew that the Christian continues to be *simul iustus et peccator*. Justification is not merely a beginning of the Christian life but a dialectical definition of every point within it. This is not simply because Christians have a way of sinning and therefore need again and again to be forgiven; it is because their righteousness is always a *justitia*

50

aliena, not their own but a δικαιοσῦνε ἐκ θεῶ, and Rom. 7:25b applies. At the same time, in accordance with the verbal ambiguity I have already mentioned, they must be at work—as the Holy Spirit certainly is at work—transforming relational δικαιοσῦνε into ethical δικαιοσῦνε, in a process that demands, but unfortunately cannot now receive, an exposition of Romans 6.

So much for the first part of this paper. God, of God's own gracious initiative, takes action through the life, sacrificial death, and resurrection of God's Son, to bring the human being, accused by the law and undoubtedly guilty, into a positive relation with Godself. If human beings are to accept this at all we must accept it in the only way open to us, as a free undeserved gift. The gift is made without qualification.

What are the consequences of this fact for Christian life, theology, and institutions? I had already determined to treat the subject in this way when my intention was confirmed by two letters which appeared side by side in *The Times* (London) on 29 January 1987. One was from Bishop P. C. Rodger. Part of it reads as follows:

> Now that justification by grace alone, received in faith, has ceased (according to the theologians) to be a matter of contention between Anglican and Roman Catholic churches ... may I express the hope that this theme will be widely preached and studied within these two communions and indeed elsewhere? For one thing, it would be good to have a question of our eternal destiny as high on the agenda as those of mainly professional-ecclesiastical interest, such as the papacy, episcopacy, or the ordination of women. For another, we need very much to bring to the attention of our society those categories of forgiveness, restoration and thankfulness, for want of which it is dying at present. . . .

Even more to my point is the other letter, from M. E. Burkill.

> ... It is sad that the Anglican-Roman Catholic International Commission (ARCIC) has only now turned its attention to justification. If the New Testament understanding of this doctrine were applied to the rest of the work of the commission, then some startling results might ensue. It would certainly alter the documents on Eucharist and ministry. Luther was so convinced of the centrality of justification by faith within Christianity that he called it the mark of a standing or falling church. It is because justification is no longer regarded as being a central theological issue that the real cause of division at the Reformation is missed. . . .

If justification is a cardinal New Testament doctrine it must be allowed a decisive role in our theological thinking and in our institutions. We may see here (though for myself I lack the specialist historical knowledge to work the matter out in detail and with confidence) a major difference between the revolutionary movement that emanated in the sixteenth century from Germany and Switzerland and the comparatively muddled and in some ways ineffective movement that originated in the eighteenth century in England. Luther recognized justification *sola gratia* and *sola fide* as the core of the New Testament and proceeded to apply it to everything: to philosophic and dogmatic theology, to theological education, to preaching, to monastic vows, to sacraments, to church order, to ethics. Wesley equally recognized justification *sola gratia* and *sola fide* as essential to the New Testament and preached it indefatigably; but he failed, perhaps because he simply was not the theological heavyweight that Luther was, to apply it systematically and consistently. The result was that the revolutionary explosive, which caused the Big Bang of the sixteenth century, went off here and there. I am not decrying this as necessarily a bad thing; it is possible to have too many major explosions; one in a millennium may be enough, and for the rest a few controlled detonations may be more effective. But I suspect that with Wesley chance—or providence?—played a greater part than control. It may even be that providence is waiting for us, 250 years on, to supply a greater measure of control.

In what remains of this paper I propose to mention rather than to discuss a number of areas in which the doctrine of justification has been or may be applied. In fact justification is, or at least is one way of formulating, the final critical and structural element in the Christian faith.

First and fundamentally we will consider the structure of the Christian life itself. I quoted earlier the old quest, *Wie krieg ich einen gnädigen Gott*? I am aware of the modern substitutes for this, and I am not unsympathetic to the human quest for a merciful fellow human, or unmindful of my obligation to be merciful to my neighbor. These valid concerns in no way antiquate or replace the old search, the old need. To anyone who believes in the existence of God no inquiry is more vital than that which asks whether this transcendent and omnipotent being is merciful. If God is not, we, who sin against God, may well say, God help us!—but God won't, for *ex hypothesi* God is not merciful and only a merciful God will deal mercifully with these rebels.

Inevitably, and rightly, we remind ourselves of 24 May 1738:

> I felt my heart strangely warmed. I felt I did trust in Christ, Christ alone for salvation; and an assurance was given me that he had taken away *my* sins, even *mine*, and saved *me* from the law of sin and death.[11]

With this we may put the following (IV. 2 in the sermon):

> Justifying faith implies, not only a divine evidence or conviction that "God was in Christ, reconciling the world unto Himself," but a sure trust and confidence that Christ died for *my* sins, that He loved *me*, and gave Himself for *me*.[12]

This twofold experience (of ordinariness and temptation) corresponds more or less with what Luther had written in the "Preface to the Epistle to the Romans," which provided the immediate occasion of Wesley's conversion. A passage commonly quoted is:

> Faith, however, is a divine work in us. It changes us and makes us to be born anew of God (John 1:13); it kills the old Adam and makes altogether different men, in heart and spirit and mind and powers, and it brings with it the Holy Ghost. O, it is a living, busy, active, mighty thing, this faith; and it is impossible for it not to do good works incessantly. It does not ask whether there are good works to do, but before the question arises, it has already done them, and is always at the doing of them. He who does not these works is a faithless man.[13]

This is sufficient to show Luther and Wesley standing on the same platform. But Luther (still in the same Preface) has more to say; for example, this:

> In this sense, then, you understand [chapter] vii, in which St. Paul still calls himself a sinner, and yet says, in chapter viii, that there is nothing condemnable in those that are in Christ on account of the incompleteness of the gifts and of the Spirit. Because the flesh is not yet slain, we still are sinners; but because we believe and have a beginning of the Spirit, God is so favorable and gracious to us that He will not count the sin against us or judge us for it, but will deal with us according to our faith in Christ, until sin is slain.[14]

In comparison with Luther, Wesley has not, I think, fully grasped the meaning of justification and its relation to the overthrow of sin. On Luther's understanding of righteousness I will allow myself one more quotation (and you may observe where Bultmann obtained some of the material I quoted earlier):

> Scripture uses the terms "righteousness" and "unrighteousness" very different-ly from the philosophers and lawyers. This is obvious, because they consider these things as a quality of the soul. But the "righteousness" of Scripture depends upon the imputation of God more than on the essence of a thing itself. For he does not have righteousness who only has a quality, indeed, he is altogether a sinner and an unrighteous man; but he alone has righteousness whom God mercifully regards as righteous because of his confession of his own unrighteousness. Therefore we are all born in iniquity, that is unrighteousness, and we die in it, and we are righteous only by the imputation of a merciful God through faith in His word.[15]

On this issue, however, Wesley does not come off badly, for he has seen (for example, at the end of the sermon) how faith cuts at the root of pride (though he has not seen, or does not show, how pride is the root of all sin). The fact is that it is by no means easy to state the relation between justification and assurance, and between justification and liberation from actual sin, in the sense of moral evil (though the latter distinction is by no means impossible, as Schweitzer and Wrede thought). Beyond their agreement in fundamentals is the fact that Wesley was a man with a tidy mind, Luther a man with a profound mind; and behind them both I should be inclined to say that Paul comes out on the side of profundity rather than tidiness. Romans 7 is in itself sufficient to show that he understood the meaning of what Luther called *Anfechtungen* (and, I would add, of what Stendahl calls an introspective conscience), and 2 Corinthians 4 and 6 underline the point in vivid language. Wesley is inclined to say that either you have faith or you do not; and if you have you know you have. If you are justified, you are on the way to sanctification and perfect love; and again these are observable and determinable matters. It is arguable, and probably true, that Christian England in the eighteenth century needed precisely this confident and clear-cut statement of a triumphant faith; but Pauline faith is not quite the same thing as Wesleyan assurance; and the connection between righteousness as a word of relation and righteousness as a moral achievement has to be worked out more delicately. The primacy of the former meaning must never be lost in the triumph of the latter. Justification is not simply the way in, but (as I have said) a definition of every point in the life of a Christian, who is never anything other than *simul iustus et peccator*. In the conversion passage quoted above the two terms that need a good deal of commentary are *assurance* and *taken away*.

I intended these observations about the Christian life to be practical and to bear upon the twin activities of preaching and pastoral care; so indeed they do, but I must leave some inferences to be drawn by others. With this we have already moved into my second point: the role of justification as a critical, structural, determining element in theology. It is all these things because it bears upon the being and nature of God. *Wie krieg ich einen gnädigen Gott?* If the Christian story is true, there is no other God than one, and mercy is the heart of God's being. "God has shut up all unto disobedience that he may have mercy upon all" (Rom. 11.32, my translation). Wesley is faithful not only to the text he is translating but to the New Testament—and above all to Paul—in the couplets that end every stanza of "Now I have found the ground."

> Whose mercy shall unshaken stay,
> When heaven and earth are fled away.
>
> Returning sinners to receive,
> That mercy they may taste and live.
>
> While Jesu's blood through earth and skies,
> 'Mercy, free, boundless mercy,' cries.

54

> Away, sad doubt and anxious fear!
> Mercy is all that's written there.

> On this my steadfast soul relies,
> Father, Thy mercy never dies!

> Mercy's full power I then shall prove,
> Loved with an everlasting love.

Wesley lacks the syllables to follow Rothe in making one whole line out of

> Barmherzigkeit, Barmherzigkeit!

but in every other respect he does full justice to the Lutheran pietist.

The doctrine of God and the doctrine of justification coinhere. This means that there is no access to God but in the witness of Scripture to Jesus Christ, and in the witness of his crucifixion and resurrection to God. Let me here briefly allude to, but not develop, another theological issue on which this observation bears. It is very nearly possible (but not quite) to set out Paul's understanding of the gospel in terms that are not theological but anthropological. In our own time we have Bultmann's existentialist understanding of Paul and John, and of this there is a kind of anticipation in a traditional Methodist understanding of the New Testament in terms of conversion and Christian experience, sometimes regarded as in themselves adequate to account for and establish Christian truth. I have certain exegetical qualifications to make (but there is not time to make them in this essay) of both these positions, but on the whole I am prepared to accept both provided that the coinherence of justification (which is the root of both Christian experience and Christian existentialism) and the doctrine of God is borne in mind. Whether we prefer to speak of anthropological theology or of theological anthropology is perhaps a matter of taste; yet it is not a matter of taste but of obligation that adjective and substantive should be held together. For Paul, and for the New Testament at large, salvation has both an existential and a cosmic dimension.

Another way of dealing with this truth will take us to the questions of canon and of hermeneutics. It may make for desirable brevity and clarity if I set out the matter with reference to Luther's treatment of the Epistle of James—so familiar that few people take the trouble to verify the facts and find out what Luther said. We must begin with what most people forget:

> Though this Epistle of St. James was rejected by the ancients, I praise it and hold it as a good book, because it sets up no doctrine of men and lays great stress upon God's law.[16]

Yet, though he thinks it good, Luther cannot believe that the epistle was written by an apostle, for two reasons:

> First: Flatly against St. Paul and all the rest of Scriptures it ascribes righteousness to works, and says that Abraham was justified by his works, in that he offered his son Isaac. . . .[17]

That is, James is out of line on justification by faith:

> Second: Its purpose is to teach Christians, and in all this long teaching it does not once mention the Passion, the Resurrection, or the Spirit of Christ.[18]

Here are the two foci on which for Luther—and I do not think Wesley would have disagreed—the message of the New Testament turns: *justificatio impiorum sola gratia sola fide*; and *solus Christus*. If we think of these as the two foci of an ellipse, they are so close together that the ellipse becomes practically a circle. This fact serves Luther as a test of apostolicity and thus of canonicity. This is perhaps not so important as it is sometimes made to appear. Luther did print James in his New Testament (though in an appendix), and those who defend the canonicity of the epistle usually do so by pointing out, on the one hand, that James uses the words justify, faith, and works in different senses from Paul (which is true), and, on the other, by pointing out concealed (and in my opinion very problematic) references to Christ. It is more important that the same criteria serve for the control of hermeneutics—not in the sense that passages in James (or elsewhere) have to be conformed willy nilly to the approved standard, and made to mean what they manifestly do not mean, but in the sense (which I have discussed in the *Festschrift* for Markus Barth)[19] that the New Testament at large is to be interpreted in terms of its center.

Finally, the biblical doctrine of justification will serve, and must be allowed to serve, as a critical and constructive element in regard to church order. It is, for example, the foundation of the doctrine of universal priesthood. There is, there can be, only one order of Christians, that of justified sinners, and in consequence there is no room for a hierarchy. If I am justified, set in a true relation with God Godself, and that by God's own decree and act, there is no higher status available to me. I need not add that this does not mean that all justified sinners will exercise the same functions, but if some are marked out to preach or to exercise pastoral care this does not constitute them a special spiritual or priestly caste to be distinguished from their fellows whose functions are different. Again, since justification is of sinners, and since we continue to need justification as long as we live, the only disqualification that excludes from the Lord's Table is the sinfulness that refuses justification and is intent upon maintaining the attitudes and practices that exclude from a true and positive relation with God. All

56

this is familiar to us in our Methodist practices and structures; therefore the obligation is much greater to maintain them—the open table, the spiritual functions of the laity, the absence of the great cleric—and to do so not by a rigorous traditionalism but by maintaining the doctrines on which they rest, remembering that these doctrines are the charter not of legalistic conservatism but of Christian liberty.

Chapter 4

REFLECTIONS ON THE CHURCH'S AUTHORITATIVE TEACHING ON SOCIAL QUESTIONS

José Míguez Bonino

When we examine the issues on which disagreement and conflict in the church have been most frequent at least during the last twenty-five years, we find that they are seldom directly related to doctrinal, jurisdictional, or liturgical questions. Conflicts within the denominations and at the ecumenical level are apt to erupt over social, economic, and political issues. While earlier struggles and divisions in the church have never been unrelated to such factors, they have now become more prominent and explicit. Churches are frequently perplexed about how to face these problems, caught in the dilemma of being irrelevant or of provoking bitter controversy and even division.

The reasons for the urgency that this problem has acquired seem to me to belong to two aspects of modern society:

The Nature of Modern Society

There is, I think, a threefold transformation characteristic of modern life and society which one could summarize in a sort of cumulative scale which is somewhat related to historical development. To put it in a simplified and over-compressed way we could say that modern life becomes increasingly *socialized*, *politicized*, and *globalized*. Human life has, of course, always been social. Personal decisions and actions have always been to a significant extent determined by social mores and conventions. But until very recently we were not clearly aware of this fact. Consequently, it was possible to conceive ethical issues as individual decisions. Churches, therefore, felt that their main ethical responsibility was to shape personal life according to Christian conviction, doctrine, or regulation. Even in dealing with issues that had a clear social matrix, ecclesiastical pronouncements and legislation tended to try to produce individual responses. Both the development of larger social units (urbanization) and the results of social sciences have made us aware of the fact that behavior is largely determined collectively. The basic process of "moralization" is concomitant with the processes of socialization. Consequently, if we want to foster certain types of ethical responses, we have to attempt to create a collective conscience that will support them. The churches have thus had to move from indications about personal behavior to "ethical teaching" for the whole society, to the articulation of a "social doctrine" that will be able to respond to the issues raised by the increasing socialization of life and to our understanding of corporate behavior.

Human life has not only become more clearly socially determined but society itself is more clearly politically organized. By this I mean that personal activity (work, education, living conditions, security, recreation) are more and more inserted into structures which are not amenable to individual decision. If we want to shape or direct them in any way, it has to be done through concerted social action and usually by means of laws, general institutions, or large scale plans. Thus, Christian conviction, if it intends to be effective, has to try to exert its influence (hopefully through means that are both effective and compatible with the faith). It is interesting to note how hesitatingly Christian theology has moved from general ethical teaching on society to areas of political and economic decision. While it felt entitled to speak with the authority of faith in areas of public morality (family, education, charity), political and economic questions appeared as governed by an autonomous reason for which it had no competence. When the churches tackle these areas, their teaching becomes more exposed to criticism—through the criticism of the structural (economic and political) mediations assumed in articulating their positions on ethical issues.

Finally, there is *globalization*. That is, the political and economic structures which so widely and deeply affect human life are more and more all-embracing geographically. This happens not only because of the growing network of communications, science and technology, exchange, transportation, international trade, transnational production, international division of labor, political blocks and spheres of influence (all of which is well known), but also because almost everybody is drawn into these networks. Some peoples and groups may be marginal in terms of the "benefits" they derive from the system, but practically nobody is anymore marginal in terms of being able to live independently of it. This transformation has led to the quest for universal guidance for human life and society. The magisterial office of the churches has been naturally drawn into this quest. It seems necessary for the churches to speak on these issues at the most universal level possible. But in a broken and asymmetrically divided world, most of what it says becomes highly controversial.

The Operation of Religious Authority

In his classic discussion of the concepts of authority, power and domination, Max Weber makes an interesting distinction between any form of "hierocratic domination," which establishes its claim by "psychical coercion, granting or refusing goods of salvation" and that form which treats the churches as "hierocratic *institutions*," the organic authorities of which "retain a claim to the legitimate monopoly of hierocratic coercion."[1] His distinction helps us to see the twofold nature of our problem. On the one hand, the question has to do with the *legitimate authority* issuing the statement; on the other, with the possibility *of ensuring the assenting reception of such a statement.*

The difficulty in dealing with this question in our time is that the relation between these two aspects of "ecclesiastical authority" has radically changed in modern times. Political and ideological changes have deprived the churches of the use of a number of objective means of coercion, both legal and social. "Authoritative statements" have lost most of their legally binding power and have become advisory. This is the case even in a church like the Roman Catholic church, with a very developed canon law which, in fact, becomes hardly enforceable outside the restricted circle of the clergy. While most churches have not seriously revised their stated doctrine and canons of authority, they function quite differently from earlier times. We urgently need a careful study—using recent sociological research—of the way in which "hierocratic power" operates in the "religious field" in relation both to civilian and political society.

To put it quite simply, church teaching, of one kind or another, can *compel* nobody except to the extent that it appeals to conscience. Not only is there no direct power (*potestas directa*) of the church, except in a very few places and circumstances, but there is no indirect power (*potestas indirecta*), which the churches used to exercise when secular governments felt under the obligation of legislating according to their teachings. The issue is even more complex insofar as there is a simultaneous plurality of different—and not seldom contradictory—ecclesiastical teachings competing for the conscience of both people and authorities. The authoritative character of a teaching, as far as its effectiveness is concerned, does not lie in the formal authority which the church may attribute to it but (a) in the social, ethical, and spiritual prestige which such a church may enjoy in the population (or in the dominant sectors of it), and (b) in the capacity of the contents of the teaching to recommend itself to the people on its own worth. Though this is obvious, churches need to be reminded of it, because they tend to give undue importance to the "intended" rather than to the "performative" (effective) authority of their pronouncements.

If this analysis is correct, "authority" depends very much on the particular characteristics of a given society and the relation of the churches to that society. The significant role that ecclesiastical pronouncements play in Latin American population can only be understood when we realize that the people retain a strong religious outlook. The "goods of salvation," to use Weber's expression, however differently understood and experienced, occupy an important place in the life of Latin American peoples. More secularized societies would react more indifferently to the church's judgments. However, it is interesting to note that even in advanced technological and supposedly secularized societies, there is a fierce struggle to obtain religious legitimation for political and economic policies. The impassioned responses— of enthusiasm or rejection—in the United States to ecclesiastical pronouncements, for instance on nuclear weapons, the economy, or foreign policy, cannot be explained unless the people involved (in many cases, governments, politicians or economic leaders whose religious practice is none too impressive) realize that such statements carry a weight in public opinion which is significant in order to obtain consensus for their policies.

The nature of that "weight" relates to the "service" which, in the consciousness of the people, the church renders to them. It seems to me that such service comprises two elements which, in different degrees and relation to each other, are always present. The fundamental one is the relation to "the transcendent," the more direct religious dimension. In this sense, a teaching can be significant if it "engages the faith," if people perceive that their relation to God is at stake in the particular issue to which the teaching refers. This, however, is also perceived through an ethical mediation: the statement rests on values and principles (human dignity and worth, justice, peace, reconciliation) which are understood to be an integral part of the religious faith. But when these values appear as autonomous, disconnected from their transcendent roots, the ecclesiastical statement loses its specific authority as such—it becomes a commonsense, philosophical, or ideological statement which may carry its own weight but which does not directly "engage the faith." This is no doubt a debatable point. I simply submit the thesis that people do not listen to the church because it is wise, good, or progressive but because, in some way, it speaks for and about God.

Finally, the effective "weight" of a teaching rests on its perceived "relevance," that is, the ability of the teaching to give expression to concerns that people feel to be significant for their lives and to offer guidance that "makes sense" in that situation. The higher interest on statements on peace in Europe and North America compared with Latin America or Africa and the reverse situation in relation to statements on social justice,

61

illustrates the point I am making. This does not mean that people's perception of the crucial questions and of sensible answers is correct. Churches may find it necessary to criticize, correct and broaden such perceptions. But they cannot discount them if they want to be heard.

Illustration from the Methodist Tradition

Teaching on social questions has been a significant part of the Methodist tradition from the beginning. It could be both interesting and profitable to trace the history of that teaching from the point of view of the style, self-understanding of the Church in relation to society, way of addressing the questions and type of reception expected and obtained. I am not competent for this job, but, as a very simple illustration, I would like to make a few comparative remarks on three such forms of teaching, taken from very diverse moments in the development of Methodism and in the historical circumstances: Wesley's "General Rules," the social creed of The Methodist Episcopal Church (1908), and the recent Pastoral Letter and episcopal "Foundation Document," "In Defense of Creation" (1986).

The very existence of the *Rules*[2] asserts the claim of the church's (in this case the Wesleyan "society's") authority to enforce on its members particular laws concerning their participation in social questions. The prohibitions to sell, buy and possess slaves, to sell, produce or consume liquor, or the rules about the transaction of business were not simply seen as pertaining to individual "virtue" but as relating to social issues (slavery, temperance, economic ethics) which had to do with "the reform of the nation." Although the rules themselves do not make it explicit, nor is the theological rationale always clear in this respect, Wesley's own treatises ("thoughts") on these issues show that the rules are related to a wider social perspective. But it is no less clear that the authority of the church is engaged through the behavior of its members. In the terms of our previous analysis we have here specific indications, meant to be followed, backed up by the disciplinary authority of the "religious society," and in turn guaranteed by the latter's capacity to "deliver or to refuse the goods of salvation."

Half a century later, the Northern Methodist Church in the United States faced the problems raised by the growth of industrial capitalism. "The Social Creed,"[3] as a responsible "social teaching" seems to be the first official document engaging the authority of the church. The shift in the nature and exercise of authority seems evident. In the first place, we have a more general sort of desiderata, not really general ethical or theologico-ethical principles but rather somewhere between what has later been called "middle axioms" (for instance, "equal rights and complete justice for all . . ." or "the principle of conciliation and arbitration") and more specific requirements ("the suppression of 'the sweating system' " or "release from employment one day in seven"). In the second place, the initial sentence defines the nature of the document: "The Methodist Episcopal Church stands—For. . . ." These are not rules addressed to individuals to regulate their social behavior; it is not in the first place teaching for the church (in fact, only later we find in successive revisions the introduction of a theological rationale and more general social teaching). It presents itself as a witness to society: the things the church "stands for. . . ." The church seems to understand itself as a moral conscience of society, speaking for justice at a particular juncture, acclaiming particularly the rights of those who stand at a disadvantage. Finally, the church places itself within society, accepts the fundamental laws of the economic and social system ("the lowest *practical point*"—for hours of labor; "the highest wage that each industry *can afford*"), and tries to humanize it, correcting "the social ills" and making harmony and peace possible.

In the recent declaration "In Defense of Creation,"[4] we are faced with a third kind of statement (even recognizing that the subject is different). In the first place, it is addressed "to all those people called United Methodist in every land"—certainly, the bishops expect the "message" to have a larger impact. But it is primarily a "teaching document" meant to engage the church in the consideration of an issue "of utmost urgency in our time." It does not claim to settle the issue but "to lead the Church in study, prayer and action"[5](from the Pastoral letter introducing the document) The bishops do not claim authority to enjoin on members a particular conduct. Nor do they intend to define officially a uniform "church stand." Rather, they invite the church to come to grips with a crucial question and provide elements for the church to grasp the facts and analyze the issue theologically and ethically. It is the teaching office of the bishops conceived as a process of mutual consultation and joint reflection. This is why it requires a clear and solid theological and ethical foundation (chapter I). In this sense, it tries to make clear why this issue belongs to the very heart of the Christian faith—in God the Creator, the Preserver, and the Redeemer. But it also requires a clear spelling out of the ethical and technical mediations. The first is discussed in terms of the issue of peace and war in the Christian tradition. The second is developed in three chapters (chs. II–IV) including both an ideological and a political analysis, buttressed with technical evidence. This explication of the mediations is a new element in relation to the first two documents and responds to the need to prove the spiritual and ethical value but also the "relevance" of the proposals. Finally, the discussion is left open in the sense of not claiming final authority. But it defines a position from where dialogue is invited: a set of concrete proposals on specific questions raised by "the nuclear crisis."

I do not now intend to discuss the substance of these documents, but from a more formal point of view to underline the change that has taken place: (a) the direct addressee—from the individual believer, to the nation, to the church as a plural body; (b) the purpose: to shape personal behavior through specific rules, to present to the nation moral orientation on some acute social problems, to engage the church in the consideration and to invite it to "covenant" for action on a critical issue; (c) the style: from a concise enumeration of rules, to more general ethical principles, to a developed theological, ethical and social argument; (d) the way of "engaging the faith": from a direct command—How is the specific command discerned? to an appeal to faith through a reasoned argument ("prayerful study"). There is continuity in the intention. There is also a significant continuity in the contents. But the three statements belong undoubtedly to different conceptions of the church's role and authority and to different expectations regarding the "reception" of ecclesiastical teaching on social questions.

Conflict in Society

However different, the kinds of teaching on social issues that we have examined share some basic presuppositions: they address society as a whole. They seem to conceive society as a body made up of different groups or sectors among which disagreement and even conflict can emerge, but which shares a fundamental consensus and functions within a fundamentally acceptable order. The social function of the church is to spot, denounce, and help to correct particular imbalances or dysfunctions (which sometimes are considered serious and urgent). Consequently, it will try to defuse or to bring down the level of conflict, to try to be objective—in some way above the conflict—in order to bring the conflicting parties to an agreement. Even strong documents like the United Methodist one on the nuclear crisis[6] or the recent Roman Catholic pastoral letter on economy[7] operate within these premises.

Can this perspective be "normative" for all ecclesiastical teaching on social questions? This question was posed at the ecumenical level by the Church and Society WCC Geneva Conference on 1966 on "The Political and Scientific Revolutions of Our Time." The title was ambivalent but the issue was not avoided. In asymmetrical societies where power is unilaterally exercised by one of the social actors (whether internal or external to that society) to the detriment of others (and even to that of the majority of the people), is it enough to look for mechanisms of compensation or is the church called to ask for a fundamental structural change? Can the church arbitrate between the parts looking for conciliation and mutual concessions or is it called to take sides and to struggle for a basic turnover in the power structure? Widely remembered is Paul Ramsey's strong criticism of the Conference in his book *Who Speaks for the Church?*[8] His explicit criticism is that in recommending specific courses of action for specific issues (for instance the Vietnam war or nuclear weapons) the Conference presupposes a decision on technical questions on which the churches have no competence. But when one looks more carefully at his argument, and particularly at his "provisional model for specific political pronounce-ments," two implicit concerns seem to be dominant. The first one is for "fairness" or balance for the opposing cases made by the different parties in discussion. It would seem that the task of the churches is to state as fairly as possible the case made by these different positions and to enunciate the middle axioms pertinent to the question but without enjoining any par-ticular position or a specific course of action. The second is to "leave" the specific decision to the "policy makers"—who have the technical know-ledge and a total view of the situation—and to offer, apart from the ethical general orientation mentioned above, the moral support of the churches. In fact it presupposes a trust in the knowledge, competence, and legitimacy of the present structure of society and its leadership to arrive at the correct decisions. In other terms, the church functions as a general moral advisor and a spiritual support of the present structure and system. Its existing checks and balances are considered adequate to cope with present challen-ges.

This is precisely one of the problems at stake today. It has become crucial for many Third World countries. Brazilian bishops (from the North-east) posed the basic problem of their society some years ago (1973) in a pastoral letter entitled, "I Have Heard the Cry of My People."[9] It runs somewhat parallel to the United Methodist one in structure: a fundamental theological statement and a careful analysis of the situation. But this leads to a radical conclusion: the rejection of the prevailing economic and political model. It is this economic model that produces the oppression of the people. Therefore "the dominated class has no other road to freedom except the long and difficult trek, now under way, in favor of the social ownership of the means of production."[10] This is the struggle of the people—not of the church. But the church does not remain neutral, as an umpire arbitrating between the different sectors, but it takes sides: "We feel that the Word of God calls us to take a stand. A stand on the side of the poor." "As in the time of Moses," say the bishops, "a people that seek to ameliorate their situation and to shake off the yoke of oppression, is fulfilling an aspect of God's designs. . . . We are convinced that it is time to opt for God and for the people."[11] The same question of "option" in conflict was faced by the churches in relation to the national liberation movements (particularly in Africa). With the support of the majority of the member churches, the WCC took the side of the liberation movements in several cases (Zimbabwe the most conspicuous) and made this option visible through symbolic financial support of certain activities (medical and educational) of these movements. The discussion was frequently sidetracked to the problem of violence. But the real heart of the controversy seems to me to hinge on two other aspects: the acceptance of a conflict that cannot be "appeased" but has to be fought through (the means is another question) and the need of the church to take sides in it. This casts the church in the role of adversary of the existing system, of a dysfunctional social actor, a role which the large Christian churches have not exercised for a long time, for which they are not prepared, and which they are very reluctant to accept.

The arguments against this option seem to overlook the fact that they actually rest on two assumptions: that the present structure of a society is fundamentally sound and able to accommodate justly the needs and rights of all its members and, therefore, that all conflicts within it can be solved by arbitration. But, in fact, in the proposed model the church, far from remaining neutral or "above the conflict," opts for the existing power structure and gives it religious legitimation. That may well be a justified decision—and it is so in many cases—but there is no theological or ethical reason to take it as "normative." The possibility that the church may have to express a negative judgment on a total system is an always present possibility. The question that it raises is again the question of criteria for such a rejection. Such criteria cannot be defined abstractly: in given situations, the very nature and form of the conflict points to the Christian concerns that are at stake. It is on this basis that the recent episcopal document defines "the defense of Creation" as the relevant criterion for the consideration of the "nuclear crisis" and comes to a total rejection of the nuclear option. The apartheid issue raised the fundamental Christian criterion of "the unity of humankind in creation and redemption" and led some churches to condemn "apartheid" outrightly as "heresy" or as determining a status confessionis. Many Latin American pronouncements on the regimes of national security have made the defense of life a basic criterion. This has led the churches to the condemnation of the national security doctrine and to a radical questioning of the operation of the economic system that has used this doctrine as its tool. When one brings together several of these criteria, one finds that they coalesce in fact in a certain "family of options" which, while leaving room for plurality, define a general direction that can help churches to test their responses to the critical dilemmas of today's world.

Unity, Partisanship, and Pluralism

There is one further issue that I would like to introduce in the discussion. Partisanship on the part of the church—that is, opting for one side, radical opposition to the existing system—seems to threaten the unity of the church. On the other hand, it seems to contradict our own argument on the way in which church authority operates today. Liberal pluralism does not solve the problem because it is itself an ideological option. The inability of liberal pluralism to deal with system-rejection betrays its limits: it operates within a certain consensus and therefore it cannot accommodate in its plurality options that challenge such consensus.

The problem should not be over-extended. There are different kinds of ecclesiastical teaching on social issues. Probably most of it does not bring up these critical options. Although issues are interrelated—and even more so in our modern complex societies—not every question demands a radical option. But some do. Is thereby the unity of the church broken? Are people "forced" on the basis of an option which they cannot share? It seems to me that this raises an ecclesiological question. What is the concrete empirical correlate of the theological reality which we call "Church"? I think that on the basis of the fundamental Protestant (and I believe also fully Methodist) conception of the church as gathered by the Holy Spirit around the proclamation and the living testimony to the gospel, one can speak of "the church," historically, as the multiplicity of ecclesiastical institutions, movements, and communities that identify themselves by reference to Jesus Christ and the gospel. But this "ensemble" must not be understood as an undifferentiated whole but as a "field," a "space," even a "battleground" in which takes place a constant "struggle for the Gospel." It is a struggle that can take the form of dialogue, debate, confrontation, or conflict which is not based on liberal pluralism because it starts from the affirmation of the specific options that it makes as valid paradigms but does not close itself to the possibility of correction, reform, and change. A specific option, undertaken in earnest, with humility, and in "prayerful study" becomes a sign raised as a witness to the Gospel, inviting dialogue, discussion, disagreement, but also calling for commitment, for the "covenanting" called for in the episcopal letter. It is an attempt to define the Church (in the specific area of the option) from the center and not from the limits. It does not say primarily who belongs and who does not belong to the church. It raises the question for all other churches and Christians to answer: can one belong to the Church and not make this option? Is not the Gospel at stake in this decision? Is this a point at which faith and unbelief part company (*status confessionis*, heresy)? It does not raise such questions as merely academic arguments but as a call—an address of faith to the Christian conscience. Naturally, not all teaching on social issues has this character. But we seem to have reached one of these crucial points in human history— a "kairos" to use Tillichian terms—when some such questions cannot be avoided.

Chapter 5

TEACHING AUTHORITATIVELY AMIDST CHRISTIAN PLURALISM IN AFRICA

Mercy Amba Oduyoye

I was still at the beginning of my teaching career when I attended an interview for the selection of Froebel teacher education grants. Even though I was at the time teaching teenage girls, I fancied myself as one who was "good with children." In response to a question as to how I would obtain and maintain discipline in the classroom, I answered confidently that I would bring my class to a point where they would behave and study well not from fear but from love. I did not get the grant. To this day I am telling myself that it was just as well, since I am still trying to discover how a person in authority can create a community of love. At twenty-two I was sure I knew the difference between fear and love. I remain convinced of the authority of love. But today it is a challenge even to try to define the terms of teaching authority.

Today I know that I do not know, but in community with others I might share my experience and derive insights from the experiences of others. I also know that a subject which the Faith and Order Commission of the World Council of Churches has seen fit to study has to be of momentous importance for the health and well-being of the churches and that none is required to provide easy solutions and conclusions. Our work in the Oxford Institute is a small ripple on the vast sea of how the church teaches authoritatively in our contemporary world and amidst Christian pluralism.

I am making a contribution to the question of authoritative teaching out of the African experience, particularly church life in Ghana and Nigeria and the ecumenical presence of the All Africa Conference of Churches (AACC).

Word from Christianity

In most of Africa, colonial and settler ambitions gave Christianity prestige and authority far out of proportion to the percentage of the population that were adherents of that faith. Colonial administrators teamed up with Western missionaries to make that happen. With political independence we now have a new factor. Countries with a confident Islamized people like Nigeria and others with a heightened cultural awareness like Zaire have effectively challenged this assumption of Christian primacy and the hegemony of Western culture. To varying degrees, this is an Africa-wide phenomenon. We can no longer assume the superiority of Western culture, the superiority of Christianity, and the superiority of the white race—not that Africans were at any point in the colonial period completely under the authority of these alien powers. Africans, especially those touched by the Western incursion, labored under a dual system. Life was governed by traditional culture and a social organization superimposed by the Western world. This dual experience continues to operate for African Moslems and Christians. We do, however, have to distinguish Christianization and Westernization at several points.

If we take Nigeria as a case, and ask the question who speaks a word from Christianity, we are confronted with such a plurality of voices that one would be tempted to give up. When Christians face state action that they find inimical to the health of the church, inter-church groups come into being to deal with the situation. At such a time all categories of churches come together and, despite the usual mutual exclusion, they manage to present a united front. The earliest examples come from the missionary period and had to do with the church's role in education. In some parts of Africa the missionaries sought the colonial government's cooperation to delegitimate traditional authority through the abrogation of cultural requirements like widowhood rites and initiation schools and interference in the norms that governed marriage and property. This strategy has continued in the post-colonial period mainly on the education front and of late in the apparent threat of Islamization. Inter-church conferences and publications have been undertaken in times of crises. Instances in Nigeria are the publication of *Christian Concern in the Nigerian Civil War*,[1] the many meetings held to debate the proposal of effecting Sharia Law in Nigeria, and the related issue of membership of the Organization of Islamic States. Like the rest of the world, Africa's reality is made up of a variety of religions, socioeconomic influences, political structures, authority patterns, and historical experiences. The complexities of interacting and interlocking systems are as overwhelming in Africa as anywhere else on the globe.

Africa, however, suffers a peculiar disadvantage. Scholars who call themselves Africanists have a tendency to exhibit interest more in Africa than in Africans, hence the proliferation of abstract statements and a lack of authentic voices of people who live and move in those structures. Our study is one more, written in the hope that it will be followed up by efforts to obtain voices from Africa, such as have resounded in the communally produced *Kairos Document* of South Africa.

Since our focus is on Christian pluralism it is necessary to reiterate the fact that there are at least two other major religions on the continent and that Christians form less than one-third of the African population. The Christian community from the Mediterranean to the Cape covers all periods of Christian history. Christianity of the first millenium has left Oriental Orthodox Christianity in Egypt and Ethiopia. The Western church of the second millenium is present in Africa in all its varieties—Roman Catholics, Lutherans, Anglicans, Methodists, Presbyterians, Baptists and others also known in the Western world. African Christianity of the future, the church of the third millenium, is already present and growing and variously labelled indigenous, independent, spiritual, etc. I have elected to apply the term African Charismatic Churches (ACC).[2] Those churches of the second millenium I call Western Churches in Africa (WCA).[3] This essay deals with the situation created by the presence of the ACC and the WCA and from the limited geographic perspective delineated above.

I also want to apply myself to a very limited area of inquiry, namely, what is their authoritative teaching and how do they teach. Given the plurality even within the different churches, statements made by their representatives in council are taken as "authoritative." The same goes for relief and rehabilitation work undertaken by the Christian Council of Nigeria after the Nigerian civil war. Though mainly composed of WCA excluding the Roman Catholics, externally it is simply "Christian action." Currently, however, the Islamic factor has thrown almost all the churches in Nigeria, ACC and WCA alike, into a new organization—The Christian Association of Nigeria (CAN). The general public accepts the words and actions of such groups as "The Christian" contribution.

As a Christian community, the scene is more chaotic as disciplinary rules and practices vary from denomination to denomination. Also the question of who has the word of authority shifts from group to group and within groups from issue to issue. This is a good point at which to examine what I am referring to as "authoritative." If I had to speak on this subject in Fante, I would have had to say "uses of power in teaching." On the other hand, if I wanted to ask for the authority figure among a group of people, I would ask for the "one who looks after them." The manner of such a person would be described as confident and fearless. The manner of a person who "knows" or who pronounces authority is assigned to or acquired by those who possess knowledge and the wisdom of experience and who speak the mind of the people. In such a situation, power and authority would have the same meaning. God in the Lord's Prayer is described as being the owner of *tumi* (power), and *Otumfo* translates to "Almighty" in Christian prayers.

However, there is a way of using the word *tumi* to connote a negative or illegitimate use of power: *atumsen*. The suggestion is that one is behaving as if one had the authority when in fact one had not been authorized. Legitimate *tumi* is authorized. The authorization comes from the group which recognizes in the person what is needed for its well-being. Performing as an *Otumfo* would have no connotation of domination; exhibiting *atumsem* would. Authority then would be the legitimate use of power by a person so recognized or assigned by a group. One may have the ability to do things or effect change but the authority to do so has to be given. I intend to appropriate the meaning of authority as legitimate power. Authority flows from a sense of responsibility as is evidenced in parenting and therefore nurtures toward maturity and self-determination.

In a society authority is assigned not only to persons but to precedence. The use of proverbs and other sources of group memory to get compliance in an African community is considered legitimate. Tradition becomes an authoritative source, and the question, "Why should I?" is responded to with "Because that is how we do things in this community." Noncompliance makes one a deviant or a heretic whom the society reserves the right to exclude or discipline. The whole society comes under the authority of its past because of what it sees as its future. Authorization for what to teach does not grow out of the base, where most people function; rather it comes from the accumulated experience of the community as interpreted by its responsible persons.

The church in Africa has authority, but that authority is seen as operative within the Christian household. Christianity has no authority over the nation and its diverse peoples who do not profess the Christian faith. It may have the power (ability, skill, knowledge) to subject the nation and specific situations to change but it has not been authorized to do so. In Nigeria, this situation became clear as churches struggled to perform humanitarian services to victims during the civil war. In ethical and moral questions as in religious beliefs and practices, one still asks the question, who speaks for the church? Christianity is organized as a very wide spectrum of autonomous communities interpreting and living out of the Bible and from a sense of history. It becomes difficult to speak of authoritative teaching of the church except in very broad terms as the authority of the Bible which represents a fundamental challenge to the whole church universal. Churches have no desire to attempt entrusting biblical interpretation to the people in the pews and enabling them to struggle to extract its meaning for their lives in the contemporary world. The authority that comes with knowledge has become the possession of those who have had formal theological education or have a place in the church's hierarchy. They create for themselves a corner in the knowledge of how to interpret the Bible, since, after all, such skills are not made available to all.

Denominations

If one discusses authoritative teaching from the point of view of churches, the issues are no less complex; they only get more focused. A church exercises authority within its congregations, not outside of them. Taking the case of the ACC in Nigeria and asking whose teaching is authoritative, we are given a long list of persons including women and men who founded churches or began single congregations, prophets and seers and pastors and healers. All who have identifiable charismatic gifts "teach authoritatively" in the church by the exercise of those gifts. They derive their authority from apostolic practice with which they claim continuity. As "ministers" of their churches and congregations, they exercise this authority. We need to know, however, that apart from persons so designated, the Holy Spirit works freely throughout the congregation making new ministers as it deems necessary. In these churches, the whole congregation as well as the individuals are open to the influence of the Holy Spirit who alone authorizes.

When I noticed how frequently Nigerian clergy would jokingly say "do as I say and not as I do," I began seriously to question the authority of persons who consciously do not practice what they preach and make a practice of that style of life. This causes me to shift my attention from who has the authority to teach to what teaching is authoritative. Churches have such a plethora of structures for decision making that any discussion of their relative positions vis-à-vis the authority issue is rather futile. In working toward an ecumenical position each church has to work realistically toward the pragmatic solution of its own structure. What teaching Christians in Africa consider or need to consider as authoritative is a more urgent discussion. For this we shall take first the case of Cameroon where the question of elitism has been raised and then South Africa where racism is the issue.

Classes

The process and strategy of evangelization has resulted in "the making of an elite" in Africa who can associate with and cooperate with the West. In the WCA, the structures, the personnel, and the interrelationships are decisively marked by the ethos of the Western churches in Europe and America. The middle-level orientation of the churches has produced an elite theology for the people. Theological concerns have focused on giving back to Africa its stolen dignity effected through the denigration of its culture and history by Western missionaries and colonizers. There has been quite an uncritical approach to this enterprise resulting in the reaffirmation of traditions that are oppressive to women and maintain the domestication of those who have lived on the margins of society as peasant farmers and artisans, and who now constitute the slum dwellers and the growing numbers of unemployed persons of the growing cities.

Using dominant structures as paradigms for christology and ecclesiology the emergent theology teaches the acceptance of hierarchial structures and pays little attention to traditional obstacles to the self-determination of women. Unaware of the plight of the rural populations, the contemporary theology from the academies and urban pulpits does not address the exploitation of rural populations by the same strategy that subjects the whole nation to the wiles of the nations north of the "money-Equator." Authoritative teaching has to be relevant. As it is, all one can say is that most contemporary theologies in Africa have no claim to authority among women and the poor of the population, rural and urban alike. It does not matter how reasoned and powerful they sound. They have no power to change the situation in which these two groups live.

Women who have observed the lack of attention to women's experience have begun to address themselves to that situation. Women cannot endorse the authoritativeness of much of what men theologians find tolerable or state simply as a matter of historical fact in terms of "this is what we do here." At a recent meeting held in Port Harcourt, women theologians grappled with issues of hermeneutics as related to the Bible and to Africa's religio-cultural corpus. They examined women's participation in the church, discussed the call of women founders of churches and the Christology embedded in women's prayers and their approach to life. What men theologians lift up as authoritative cannot be blindly endorsed by women.

From Cameroon has come a powerful critique of the concentration on culture to the exclusion of other social realities, like global North-South economic relationships and their local version. Others in Eastern Africa have pointed to the lack of political analysis which, together with the economic analysis, make contemporary African theology irrelevant to the majority of the people and therefore lacking in authority. Jean-Marc Ela, using the paradigm of the Eucharist, asks whether it is related to salvation or to dependence in Africa. True to African culture, Jean-Marc begins with a story. But what a story:

> ... thousands of peasants are being forced to pull up millet that is just sprouting and to plant cotton in its place. ... It is all done so quietly, under the watchful eye of the agricultural monitors employed by a large development company investing in cash crops.[4]

74

If this does not recall the building of Pithom and Rameses (Exod. 1:6 –14), I do not know what does.

The piece describes the peasants as "landless peasants." If this had happened in Ghana, I would have said persons "rendered landless," for throughout Africa multi-nationals are buying people off their lands; and to a lesser extent rural people, unable to survive in the economic chaos, sell bits of land to those of their own people who have access to loans and can therefore attempt modern farming methods. Like their nations, rural people in Africa have become increasingly "sucked into the game of unequal exchange."[5] Contemporary African theology that does not address this situation cannot be authoritative for the people whose experience Ela describes. If culture is anything to go by, their "theologians" would be encouraging them to resist, as it is against the gods to destroy a food crop. They would stop this sacrilege as Yahweh put an end to the sacrifice of children. To be authoritative is to monitor the changing face of oppression and empower persons for their liberation. We shall be *doing* the Eucharist rather than *saying* it. Remembering Christ would become a concrete act of enabling the feeding of thousands. The bread would come from their own millet. Ela projects the church in Africa as a "dependent church among oppressed peoples." Teaching authoritatively will include the reading of the Good News and its interpretation by the oppressed people. A powerful exposition of the same Good News from the perspective of those who do not share the peasants' experience or take it into consideration cannot be considered authoritative by them. It can neither help transform the socio-economic situation nor nurture the human relations within it as long as it does not assign much worth to the lives of the people it is attempting to teach. There is no excuse for "irrelevant" theology from academia, but there is even less for authoritarian teaching from the pulpits of African churches.

Ela lays upon the church in Africa "the urgency of rooting the Christian message in Africa's realities" and "the renunciation of all forms of compromise and complicity with current regimes." Teaching authoritatively will have a curriculum that touches "the privileged of the system (who) are stifling their consciences to protect their situation." Teaching authoritatively will include a call to action in respect of liberation from oppression which is "the locus of our rediscovery of the gospel nature of the Church."[6] The authoritative teaching of Ela comes from the fact that he has himself become part of the "damned of the earth" by taking up a rural ministry. His is the authority that arises out of "bonding." It is the authority of love.

Moving southward in Africa, teaching authoritatively means confronting by word and action the heresy of apartheid and the demonic racist structure that it operates. If there is one place in Africa where the issue of teaching authoritatively is crucial and urgent it is South Africa. This is a situation that demonstrates in bold lines how from the same religion and its scriptures both oppressive and liberating attitudes and structures can arise. Which of the many teachings can we label as authoritative, and would what is authoritative for blacks be authoritative for whites?

Faced with a system designed to guard the privileged life-style of a minority from change, how effective is authoritative teaching that comes from the ranks of those who are poor, oppressed, and with no state machinery? What authority do the powerless exercise? The prophetic theology option has the authority of the few whites who have renounced apartheid and the blacks who believe the country has a chance to redirect its course on an interracial ideology. But there is black theology, whose authority is in its emphasis on the prior recognition of the humanity of black people if prophetic theology is to become authoritative for all the races of South Africa. What are the chances of teaching authoritatively in the midst of intransigence, and what is the authoritative word?

A study of the history of apartheid shows how a minority people fearing for their own safety and appropriating the story of the Exodus, the conquest and settlement of Canaan, and protestant doctrines of election and damnation, have got themselves into a situation of "we and none else" unless they exist to serve our interests. The pro-apartheid whites who have the state apparatus on their side exercise power but their authority is challenged by the blacks and the few whites in the ranks of the anti-apartheid struggle.

The government's lack of authority is too evident to warrant mention. This is inevitable because the economic, political, military strength of the state is not being used for change that will result in a higher standard of life for blacks. Discipline in terms of "State of Emergency" (1961) and "State of Unrest" (1985) is coercion toward compliance with inhuman situations. Apartheid becomes demonic and destructive as power is divorced from love, the creative and nurturing matrix of human relations. If the church's teaching is to be authoritative it will have to seek a practical route of exorcising the demon.

The South African government lacks authority because it is not geared toward building one nation but rather has created dependent states within its borders. It has created a house divided against itself, the very antithesis of John Skinner's understanding of a community that can operate authoritatively, that is, one that nurtures and shapes its members into relatively free persons "resulting in a mutual interdependence which does not occasion pathological dependence but healthy freedom. . . ."[7]

Teaching authoritatively in South Africa will have to come and does come from those whose theology is based on "the unquestionable Right to be Free," the South African theology that arises out of concrete struggles against affliction that several groups have embarked upon. Theology that takes none of this into account cannot speak authoritatively in South Africa. Theological content would become meaningful as action and reflection are coordinated to bring about effective change. Unlike the West African elitist and sexist examples, South African theologians seek to address their situation in its totality, from academia, church, conference halls, and streets. Moreover much of the theology is being shaped in societal contexts. This brings me to the question, How does the church teach authoritatively?

Methods of Authoritative Teaching

Sennett describes the methods of two orchestra conductors, one whose baton you can hardly see and the other who even throws it at the musicians to get them to perform appropriately.[8] Our contemporary experience of authoritative teaching in our academies as in African culture approximates the latter style and is no model for the church. Apart from the irrelevance of much of the content, the methods are basically authoritarian and domesticating. My youthful dream of authority through loving relations among participants in a community of learning remains a dream. The education machineries have little use for mutuality. Learners and teachers are two classes of people. Messianic attitudes of political leaders and authoritarian methods of "bosses" continue to cripple the system and to stifle creativity.

In the church teaching is understood as bearing witness to the gospel in the form of proclamation. "Doing" the gospel is a secondary aspect. But teaching of the church's faith and tenets is often more effectively transmitted and caught through the liturgy which the church undertakes as a corporate body. More often, however, what does get designated as authoritative are formally promulgated rules concerning moral agency. The result of this approach is that instead of an interdependence, characteristic of a "learning community," a permanent state of immaturity is fostered. There is an unspoken fear that a variety of approaches, opinions, and structures would jeopardize the unity of the Christian community and the authority of its leaders, hence a cadre of persons is designated as the authentic interpreters of what the church stands for.

Teaching in the church is still from pulpit to pew. In Nigeria there is an assumption that those who mount the pulpit know better than those who sit in the pews and there is constant anxiety that the "pews are becoming higher than the pulpit." It is an excellent idea to have a well-educated ordained ministry but this stated reason is insupportable. It is a sign that the egalitarianism of God's kingdom (Matt. 23:8–12) has not yet penetrated the mentality of the Christian clergy.[9] Teaching authoritatively must have sharing and participation woven into its style. The assumption must be that everyone has something to offer just as the trained theologians offer their skills of exegesis, etc. There is in Africa a conspiracy of silence over all forms of interpretations of the Bible except the literal and the spiritualizing, that enables hierarchical and domineering styles to prevail.

The paternalism put in place by missionary strategy has little reason to exist today but it does, and it goes together with the patriarchal system that hands down knowledge in a hierarchical manner and treats it as a patrimony reserved for the few who claim direct succession to the teachers of the ancient church. Everybody else is to be protected from possible heresy. The handing down is selective not only in terms of what is handed down, but also to whom. This false love is afraid of partnership and is designed to lead to deeper and permanent dependence. That it has taken so long for African Christian theology to see its way into the print media is evidence of how successful but devastating paternalism can be.

Authority of moral and ethical injunctions does depend for credibility on the style of life of those proposing the injunctions. Those who purport to dispense authoritative teaching by word should at least refrain from excusing themselves from teaching by deed. Yet leaders of thought in the church continually claim exceptions by the way they live. Those who would promulgate laws from above should not hold themselves above the law, notwithstanding what we all know very well, namely, that "the authorities in the Church cannot adequately reflect Christ's authority because they are still subject to the limitations and sinfulness of human nature."[10] Flouting the injunctions they give others with no sign of remorse undermines not only their authority as persons and proclaimers of God's will; it also casts doubts on their claim to have stood in the council of God.

The Future of Teaching

In her trilogy on the Christian community, Letty Russell[11] wrestles with the question of how we can live the future today, claiming our memory of the future as our authority for what we do and say now. Those who would teach must be ready to learn, for it is what develops from the base that gets authentic reception as authoritative by the community. We cannot allow prejudice to cheat us of the wisdom of those who are different from us. Since the church is a *koinonia*, the style of sharing has to apply to all aspects of its life. We are to participate in discerning, formulating, and acting upon what is authoritative, always attentive to the biddings of the Holy Spirit and our future as God's children. We do not know what it will look like, but we know we shall be new creatures in a new creation—the old is passing away.

Authority in the church must not become like the rule of the principalities and powers of this world. Like the kingdom which is not of this world, the church's teaching ministry is only legitimate as it results in freeing people and in building a just society. Participants in the church's life have a right to refuse recognition to teaching that is designated to subject them to tyranny. On the other hand, if what is taught empowers their struggle, as Jesus worked to have Galilean peasants struggle for a better life, then it is authoritative teaching. But if it fosters ahistorical ideals to salve the conscience of exploiters, then it is an illegitimate use of power.[12]

Teaching authoritatively should be put in the context of the larger society of which the church is a part. So a mutuality of learning and teaching would be an appropriate style to cultivate. The church cannot decide which of its tenets and teachings would be appropriated by those inside it, let alone those "outside." People decide what is authoritative by what effect it has on the general community and on themselves as persons. We cannot assume that people will simply go along with the consolation "it is for your own good." They are going to determine for themselves what is good for them. So a consensus must be sought at all times if teaching is to be authoritative. For the poor and exploited, the future does not include their present conditions, therefore no teaching will be authoritative which requires them to cooperate with such a present.

If we can conceive authority as possible for all who participate in the church, we can see authoritative teaching as God's gift as much to women as to men. In view of Paul's "household tables" an African woman once said to me, "Why do we listen to Paul when he talks about things of which he knows nothing? Where was Paul when women followed Jesus and sat at his feet? Where was Paul when women stood at the foot of the cross? Where was he when Jesus made women the apostles of his resurrection? The trouble is by the time he arrived on the scene all he saw was men having a talking session. At any rate," she concluded, "didn't the Bible say the old is passing away?" If the church is to see itself as a household of authority, it cannot ignore women's teaching skills and their insights into what is to be taught and how. We have to agree with Letty Russell that there is need to "keep open the possibility that God is doing a new thing; and this new thing may have to do with the way we exercise authority in God's world household, the *oikos* of God (Jer. 31:22)."[13] The bifocal structure of traditional Africa used to ensure that the women's perspective was not lost. Today new ways are being suggested to augment this invaluable perspective.

The charismatic gift each has is held in trust for the whole community; by exercising it we add to the community's power to survive, grow, and perform. It is through our charisma that God's authoritative teaching will be communicated. We therefore cannot afford to marginalize anyone or install authoritarianism on the throne of the Holy Spirit. As ARCIC has observed, "to arrive at a wider *koinonia* we need humility, charity and a willingness to learn."[14] This applies not only to confessional families but to the smallest unit of the Christian community. These qualities that annul fear and install faith in our bilateral confessions should accompany our methods of teaching authoritatively.

Africa

Apart from statements of ecumenical bodies and of the episcopal conferences of the Roman Catholics in Africa, there have been few authoritative statements put out by churches and church leaders in connection with societal issues. The WCA by and large follow "the deposit of faith" left by their Western missionaries and endorse the agreements of their confessional families. Since very few of such issues touch African realities and those that do are either too vague or too specific, national churches can afford to ignore them and they generally do. Thus their authority patterns, issues, and methods have remained dependent on their past. There is very little to refer to that one can describe as their authoritative teaching. What there is comes in the form of Bishops' charges and presidents' addresses—all can only be authoritative to the extent to which the flock recognize their own conclusions in them. ARCIC describes such authorities as those who have responded more fully to the call to minister "by the inner quality of their life, [and thus] win a respect which allows them to speak in Christ's name with authority." Their authority is pastoral.

The AACC has remained at this point within the oral tradition. What is in print is mostly the studies which scholars of the WCA have made of the AACC. As their own scholars begin to write not simply to chronicle their origins but to explicate their theology and ethics, we may learn something further on how they teach authoritatively beyond being the direct channels for the guidance of the Holy Spirit, which is a form of authoritative teaching that highlights the aspects of mutual responsibility and interdependence. Their approach reinforces the contemporary women's call to more inclusiveness, although these churches themselves have not completely arrived at this point.

With the prodigious memories of a people of an oral culture, quoting the Bible as authority has become very common and used in the same way as proverbs and myths and folk tales have been utilized in teaching and in socialization. The ARCIC statement concludes that to Christ, God has given all authority in heaven and on earth and that Christ bestows the Holy Spirit to create a communion of men [sic] with God and with one another. Profound and careful as such statements are, their appropriation by those who have not been a part in creating them is to reinforce their traditional proof-texting approach to the Bible and their denominational histories and practices.

What is lacking in my opinion is the application of the principle of "shared commitment" in the task of creating "a common mind in determining how the gospel should be interpreted and obeyed."[15] African Christians agree that by the action of the Holy Spirit the authority of the Lord is active in the church. What is lacking is the communal approach to discerning where and in what way the Holy Spirit is acting; also absent is the concern for what God is doing in the margins of society and from within the suffering of people in history. For a culture that boasts of strong family ties and a communal approach to life, the inability to apply it in and to the Christian community is a very serious factor in any deliberations on African Christianity.

There is also a marked lack of evidence that the participation of the WCA in the world bodies to which they belong have had much effect on how or what the churches teach authoritatively. It is only in recent times that "authoritative statements" are being made on apartheid and even more recently has the issue of polygamy been placed on a world agenda. The African churches' role in evolving authoritative teaching in the communion of churches is very nebulous, some would even say marginal if not marginalized. The churches that are based in a continent with a phenomenal growth of Christianity should be seen to be affecting the shaping of the church's authority in matters of faith. It is an obligation which is not being fulfilled.

Contemporary deliberations on teaching authoritatively in the church has been limited to theological matters, notably baptism, eucharist, and ministry promoted by the Faith and Order Commission of the WCC. Juridical authority remains in the traditional modes and molds. The "conciliar" structures of African churches have played even more marginal roles in the promotion of these discussions. Unable to maintain the cumbersome structures put in place for them on the pattern of Western ones, theological commissions and consultations on church life have naturally taken second place to those of church service. Often, of course, implementation has balked at the level of those who actually teach with authority in the churches.

Teaching authoritatively amidst Christian pluralism in Africa becomes not an academic issue but one that can become a stumbling block for effective action by churches and Christians on matters of life and death.

81

Decisions by churches and Christians are by nature theological, making the lack of theologically alert churches a very dangerous handicap for Christian effectiveness in Africa.

I have guided us through the plural nature of Africa's realities and the even more diverse expressions of Christianity in Africa. I have tried to convey my sense that the church's word to Africa is more often self-serving rather than oriented towards participating in exposing, challenging, and changing the plight of the poor and exploited. Having lost much of the prestige that was associated with being the religion of the Western powers in Africa, the church has begun to play a defensive game failing even to have much influence on political leaders who are Christians, not to speak of the business world that is a front for the death-dealing power of Western capitalism and militarism in Africa. The church hesitates to make statements on political and economic issues. What goes on in churches and congregations with regard to who teaches authoritatively is simply a local variety of a global problem, the issue being how far the churches are willing to turn away from authoritarianism, paternalism, and patriarchy to communal participation and partnership in decision making, in learning and teaching. Teaching authoritatively today calls us to become a learning community that is receptive to what the Spirit is communicating to Africa and to the whole world.

Chapter 6

CONSENSUS AND RECEPTION

G. R. Evans

"For many years I have been tossed by various winds of doctrine, exclaimed John Wesley."[1] "In this labyrinth I was utterly lost, not being able to find out what the error was, nor yet to reconcile this uncouth hypothesis either with Scripture or common sense."[2] ". . . when they interpreted Scripture in different ways I was often much at a loss."[3] Wesley was able to cut through his intellectual perplexities in a moment of trust when his heart was "strangely warmed," and the course of his life was changed. He was able afterwards to rely on his insight and to understand his faith in the light of it. But he was also aware that personal experience is not enough. The Christian life is not to be lived in solitude. "You must have some companions in the way; for how can one be warm alone?"[4] The companionship of the Christian community is a shared experience, which extends to our understanding of our faith.

At the time when Wesley was still searching for certainty, he came across Vincent of Lerins' dictum about consensus: *quod ab omnibus, quod ubique, quod semper creditum* (what has been believed everywhere, always, and by everybody). He found the underlying principles helpful, but he soon discovered practical difficulties about seeking for a faith held by all Christians everywhere and always. He notes the danger of getting "antiquity" out of balance with Scripture, misunderstanding the evidence of the past, imputing universality to local decrees and failing to take account of contemporary circumstances.[5] Here he was heir in part to a debate which had arisen with some vigor in the sixteenth century, and which has had significant consequences for the shared understanding of our faith until the present.

In the preface which he wrote to the *Acta* of the meeting in Ratisbon in 1541,[6] Melanchthon proposes a theory of the Church's teaching authority. The Ratisbon article *de potestate interpretandi Scripturae* has, he explains, three prongs. It equips the Church with the "power of interpreting" envisaged on a human model (*humano more*), that is, on an analogy with the magistrate's authority to interpret the law. It does not allow that individuals or a minority can correct the judgment of the majority, nor dissent from their view. It asserts that the decrees of Councils must be obeyed. Melanchthon's primary objection is to the transference of a political frame of reference to the Church. He had made the same point in Article 28 of the Augsburg Confession.[7] In a kingdom the king or magistrate has the power to interpret law. And this authority must be obeyed. A magistrate's rules and opinions are valid as reasonable judgments of one to whom God has entrusted an office.[8]

In the church things are very different. "Let us set aside for a moment that image of a human polity, and think of a dispersed community which truly calls on God, is governed by the Holy Spirit, spreads the pure doctrine of the Gospel and is defended amidst dangers by wonderful works of God." In this *coetus* (assembly) power is not fixed in certain persons or a certain group,[9] but is a gift to some; it is a gift of divine light by which they understand the wisdom handed down in the gospel. There is a huge gap (*ingens intervallum*) between this gift and that "magistrate's power" which is attributed to bishops or councils.[10] Those individuals who have the mandate of God (*mandatum Dei*) must speak up against the majority opinion and against errant rulers. Luther dared to do it. Our congregations (*nostrae ecclesae*), says Melanchthon, follow him rather than the *consensus* of so many centuries, popes and academics.[11]

The question of what is duly constituted authority in establishing doctrine was a particularly vexed one in the last medieval centuries and the Reformation period. Writing on the Thirty-nine Articles of the Church of England in 1579–8, Thomas Rogers speaks of the notion of an "ordinary power annexed to the state and calling of popes, bishops and clergyman,"[12] which guarantees right interpretation and right teaching. Luther had argued, along the same lines as Wyclif, that no such special power is bestowed with orders, and the people of God in their local congregation have the right and the power to judge all teaching.[13] Indeed, it is the duty of a Christian congregation to resist impositions upon them contrary to the teaching of Scripture.[14] Rogers, like Melanchthon, believes that "to interpret the word of God is a peculiar blessing, given by God only to the Church and company of the faithful, though not to all and every one of them."[15]

The threads of Melanchthon's argument are familiar enough in the debates of the sixteenth century to be individually unremarkable. But when he weaves them together he creates a fabric in which the strains can clearly be seen. His first concern, which he makes the warp of the material, is to get away from the civil and political model, with its implications that power is something imposed from above and that authority goes with office and order. The difficulty of rethinking these assumptions even in the secular sphere is evident in the *Landesordnung* of the Tyrolean revolutionary Michael Gaismair (1526): "You will . . . act in unity and always by mutual decision," he says, but also "You will faithfully obey the authority set over you."[16] Melanchthon calls for a rethinking of the nature of the Christian community itself, and therefore of the quality of authority within it. Here, too, difficulties presented themselves early on. In a notable comment on Luther's progression, one modern Lutheran scholar remarks:

> Even as Luther had, in his struggles with the fanatics and sectarians, recognized the impossibility of turning over the Church, like the civil government, to "Mr. Everyman," so he now recognized also the deeper reason as far as the Church is concerned. The Church does not exist as a result of the goodwill of the believers but solely because of the real presence in word and sacrament of the exalted Christ, who has authoritatively set the ministry of proclaiming the word in opposition to the authority of "Mr. Everyman."[17]

Melanchthon was as wary as Luther would soon become of mass, majority, or mob rule in Christian as in civil communities. He gives the authority in interpretation and doctrinal decision making to the few who are called by God and not to the community as a whole. But that leads him into contradiction of a position he states in one of his sermons. That *coetus* is catholic, he says, which embraces the *consensus* of the Church.[18] The *doctrine* of the word of God which we embrace is that to which "the Church bears witness."[19] In Melanchthon's preface to the Ratisbon *Acta* the truth into which the Holy Spirit has led German Christians through Luther is set over against the *consensus* of a majority of Christians over the centuries.

The root of the problem was that the dictum of Vincent of Lerins was being put under intolerable stress by recent events. Melanchthon could not have subscribed in 1541 to the statement of a recent twentieth-century Lutheran-Roman Catholic Commission, that "a theological teaching remains a theory of individuals as long as it is not affirmed and adopted by the whole people of God."[20] It is on the point of *consensus* that we come to the weak place in his fabric.

What is the authority of consent? Aristotle saw it as a principle of verification.[21] For Euclid and Boethius alike, the *communis animi conceptio* is a truth attested by universal acceptance.[22] In Christian doctrine there is an ultimate test in Scripture. The Christian community cannot by its *consensus* overrule the Word of God.[23] But when it is in harmony with God's Word it has a force which is of an altogether higher order than the sort of *consensus* Cicero envisaged as an indication that what all peoples accept is natural law.[24] Hincmar of Rheims in the ninth century sees it as a sign of the unity of the communion of the church that there should be consent and *consonantia*.[25] Thomas More speaks of the *consentientis authoritas*, the authority of consent, and Erasmus thinks it wrong to dissent from the *sententia consensuque Ecclesiae*.[26] The general principle is not in dispute in the sixteenth century. But pointing to universal consent was another matter in an age when there were rival claimants to be the "true Church" and it had become a commonplace of polemic that the leaders of the Church of Rome had sought to impose false teaching on the people of God for their own ends. The three criteria into which Vincent of Lerins broke down the notion of universal consent: time, place, and unanimity are all seen as important in a recent definition of reception by the Lutheran Church in America. Reception is described as "a process involving all parts of the Church, all believers" and as taking place over time.[27] All three are discussed in the sixteenth century debates.

The first and most obvious sense in which the dictum was being tested concerns "place." Luther argued for the importance of the local congregation, a community (*gemeyne*) in which the pure gospel is preached.[28] Thomas More, in his *Responsio* to Luther, says that the Church of God is one (*una est ecclesia Dei*) and those who separate themselves from it, even if they form a congregation, can be no more than a *conciliabulum diaboli* (council of the Devil).[29] He describes an enquirer, "E," who sets out to verify what he hears preached in one local church by travelling through many Christian nations to see if he finds everywhere "the same faith, the same teachings regarding what is necessary for salvation."[30] If Luther says that the Christians of Italy, Germany, Spain, France, and so on are outside the Church, he is either arguing that the church is nowhere, or, like the Donatists, he is reducing it to a gaggle of two or three heretics whispering in a corner.[31] But More concedes that it is not easy to find a "perfyte perswasyon and byleve" which is "receyved thrughe crystendom," although Christians in many places may concur.[32] The argument from what is received everywhere had, for practical purposes, temporarily broken down, and the best which can be advanced by way of warrant from ubiquity is some such formula as "Hereunto subscribe the churches in Helvetia, Wittemberg, Bohemia,"[33] or that this is "the judgment of our godly brethren in foreign countries."[34]

In the case of time we come up against Luther's contention (endorsed vigorously by Calvin),[35] that "in the matter of judging teachings" one "should not care at all about . . . old precedent, usage, custom"[36] even if it "lasted a thousand years."[37] The kind of thing he had in mind is More's argument that the cult of saints and images which has been allowed for generations by common consent is warranted by usage, and that this custom is a stronger proof even than miracles that such worship is right.[38] More argues in reply that Christians are bound by the past. Where past generations have arrived at consensus we must remain true to their position, however many now want to abandon it.[39] He cites Augustine's view that what is held by the whole Church as a matter of invariable custom is rightly held to have been handed down by apostolical authority.[40] In a later generation the English recusant Edmund Lechmere insisted that we must follow "the direction of the Church... which all times could point at."[41] More looks to find continuity from the time of Christ's Passion *in haec usque tempora* (even to the present time), the Church remaining in unity of faith *per tot secula* (through all generations).[42] Luther's community is not only a "rivulet" flowing away from the universal church but a break in continuity. Where does Luther think the church has been in the ages before him? When in the past have Luther's views been the church's views.[43] Nowell, in his Catechism of the 1570s speaks of "custom" as "at this day received in our churches" as something derived from "the ordinance of the apostles and so of God himself."[44]

This shake-up of assumptions about continuity of *consensus* in time forced new thinking which has borne fruit since. In More's *Dialogue* there is already some recognition that opposing views may have coexisted in the church for centuries and then merged in a single voice which must be heard as that of Christ. For that reason a recent consensus may be no less binding than an old one. "Yf there were any thyng that was peradventure such that un the chyrche sometyme was doubted and reputed for unreveled and unknowen; yf after that the holy chyrche fall in one consent upon the one syde eyther by common determynacyon at a generall counsayle or by a perfyte perswayson and byleve... receyued thrughe crystendome" it is established as Christian truth.[45] In a notable nineteenth century usage of the term "reception" Pusey spells out one implication in a letter to Manning. The Council of Trent "might," he postulates, "by subsequent reception, become a General Council." That would mean that "it might be so now virtually, although 'as yet' unrecognized as such by the whole Church, but in a state of suspense."[46] A simpler expression of the same idea, with a broader application, is to be found in the Final Report of ARCIC I. The process of reception may be "gradual" (that is, running through time) "as ... decisions come to be seen in perspective through the Spirit's continuing guidance of the whole Church."[47]

A similar shaking out of assumptions is to be seen in the case of the principle of unanimity. Wyclif states comfortably that it is the nature of every creature to know God to be his *superior* and to want to help other creatures to work together as one.[48] More describes the Holy Spirit's method of bringing about *consensus* among his people, as he "enclyneth thyr credultye to consent in the byleuying all in one poynt whiche is the secret instyncte of god."[49] Heretics do not disrupt this pattern, for their dissent is transient in the continuing history of the church.[50] Nor is it necessary for all Christian people to be present to vote in order to register their consent. A council is the church in microcosm; we cannot all meet but we can do so through our representatives.[51] But against this picture of a community in concord we need to set More's assertion that in no action of a multitude is unanimous consent required.[52] Edmund Lechmere goes further. The truth of the community's assertions, he says, "dependeth not upon the approbation of everie one that is in her communion . . . if some of them do chance to forgoe the truth and leave it, there is power in the rest to define the matter and condemn them."[53] The existence of dissenters is no serious threat to the principle of consent if Lechmere is right, and indeed the church had got along well enough in the confidence which he and More expressed, namely, that the wrong view will simply be outvoted. But as we saw in Melanchthon's discussion of the Ratisbon *Acta,* the Reformers were breaking with tradition in claiming that it may sometimes be the case that an individual or a small group is mandated by God to speak the truth against centuries of accepted teaching and a majority view in the church. In a philosophical treatise on establishing certainty, a sixteenth century *Grammar of Assent*, Sebastian Castellio criticizes Lutherans and Calvinists for wrong thinking on this point.[54] And the Reformers questioned in the same breath the idea that Councils speak for the community and therefore represent the consensus of the majority in their decrees.[55]

These breaks with what we may call the three "unities" of time, place and unanimity in the understanding of reception created difficulties because of the underlying assumption Lechmere voices when he speaks of "power in the rest to define the matter." He implies that the *consensus* of the community is not merely an indication where the truth lies, a principle of verification in the Aristotelian and Ciceronian sense, but a creator or legitimizer of truth. The Final Report of the first Anglican-Roman Catholic International Commission suggests that reception "does not create truth or legitimize the decision." Rather "it is the final indication that such a decision has fulfilled the necessary conditions for it to be a true expression of faith."[56]

This is of some importance in the light of a picture of Christian authority which has begun to emerge in recent ecumenical discussions. A central conception of *koinonia* in the New Testament sees it as a communion of individuals who have a relationship to Christ as their head and a relationship to one another which is dependent on that primary relationship.[57] That sets at the very center of the Church's being a unifying structure formed by living relationships, out of which proceeds all Christian ministry. Because its source is God himself, this ministry is authoritative. Jesus spoke of his Father as the one who has sent him into the world and gave him authority. He himself entrusted that authority to his disciples as he sent them out in their turn (John 16:4, 27 and 17:2, 18, 20–21). The sending is also a commissioning, a gift of authority to do the work which is needed (John 20:21–3). The essence of authority thus derived is that it is never cut off from its source. God's authority flows into the world perpetually through his people in the continuing life of the church.[58]

The ordained ministry, and *a fortiori* those who have a ministry of oversight, are part of the community. They have authority "within" and "among" the Christian faithful, and "over" them only from "within."[59]

These new elements in the understanding of Christian authority make a significant difference to the relatively crude model with which sixteenth century thinkers were working when they debated power and jurisdiction. And they have important implications for the concept of *magisterium* (to use an anachronistic term) and the question of authority in the church's structures of decision making in matters of faith on which the Ratisbon talks came to grief and with which we have seen sixteenth-century thinkers struggling.

Wyclif assumes with the majority of medieval scholars that one and the same truth is taught by Christ and the apostles, by the Fathers and by General Councils, and that it is not only *recta* (right) and *eadem* (consonant) but also complete.[61] Details may be explained as controversies make it necessary, but Christian truth is essentially fixed and finite. As Nowell puts it in his Catechism of 1570, "it were a point of intolerable ungodliness and madness to think, either that God hath left an imperfect doctrine, or that men were able to make that perfect, which God left imperfect." On this view, councils and ecclesiastical assemblies and preaching "serve either to the expounding of dark places of the word of God, and to take away controversies that rise among men" or "to the stablishing of the outward governance of the Church."[61] On this basis distinction was widely made among the reformers between additions which carried only human authority and the central truths to which nothing could be added,[62] which encouraged a separation of human and divine in the Church's authority, and it was argued that there could be no obligation for any Christian to accept the former. Again, we are dealing with a relatively crude model. These points were insisted on by Reformers in an age when it seemed that ecclesiastical authority was seeking both to add to Christian truth and to impose on Christian people the duty to believe what was added. The fight for gospel truth, for apostolic simplicity, went on everywhere in reforming communities.

The concept of an authority flowing always and directly from God through his church and acting from within the body of the faithful puts these anxieties in a different light. Truth is recognized by the people of God where they "discern a harmony between what is proposed to them and the *sensus fidelium* of the whole Church," on the one hand, and "the apostolic faith," on the other hand,[63] and that perception is made possible by the action of the Holy Spirit. Whether the definition is framed by a council or a primate or a commission or an individual, and formally accepted by a democratic vote, whether unbroken historical continuity can be established, whether the formulation has been accepted all over the world, are important indications, but they do not create truth or legitimize a decision or in themselves authorize its acceptance.

The nature of Christian authority is such that it "involves" rather than "imposes on" minds and hearts. The notion of reception as an active welcoming rather than a passive acquiescence is adumbrated in the Middle Ages. The conception of an active "receiving" is put forward in the eleventh century by Anselm of Bec. In his *De Casu Diaboli* he tries to answer the question how some angels were able to persevere in righteousness while others were not. If God gave some perseverance and not others, it would seem that he condemned some to fall, and that would make him the author of evil. Anselm's explanation is that God gave perseverance to them all, but only some accepted it; that is, it was by their own active response that they received it.[64]

Although the word "receive" was in use in the sixteenth century in the general area of what we should now call "reception,"[65] it was not yet a fully established technical term. But the notion of an active "embracing" is clearly present. "In general councils, whatsoever is agreeable unto the written word of God we do reverently embrace."[66] "Whatsoever also is grounded upon God's written word, though not by our common and vulgar terms to be read therein, we do reverently embrace."[67] "We must not only hear and understand . . . but also with steadfast assent of mind embrace . . . heartily love . . . yield ourselves desirous and apt to learn, and to frame our minds to obey."[68]

The essence of this "active welcoming" is that it is not an individual but a collective act of the people of God. It shifts the recent emphasis of the word *consensus* from its use in, for example, Aquinas, where it is merely an agreement of the will to sin or to marriage and so on, to the idea of shared understanding: *con-sensus*. Thus Melanchthon is able to define the church as: *homines amplectentes Evangelium*,[69] people collectively embracing the gospel. In the same spirit the Church of England's Thirty-nine Articles urge that the creeds "ought *thoroughly* to be received and believed."

This embracing is not only a consent of the believing mind and heart, as it were, a warm hug of faith; but an exercise of judgment. Again, the idea is present in embryo in the sixteenth century, but colored by an anxiety about the dangers of letting inferiors judge their rightful rulers. It is not popular, says Wyclif, for the people to judge (*populum iudicare*), especially for them to judge ecclesiastical authority.[70] The question of judgment is inseparable in Luther's view from the dispute about "imposition" by duly constituted authority. What Thomas More calls the *ecclesiae iudicium in fidei causa* (judgment of the church in matters of faith)[71] involves for Luther judgment by the congregation. He argues from I Thessalonians 5:21 that Paul does not want to see any teaching or decree obeyed unless it is examined and recognized as good by the congregation which hears it. "Test everything but hold fast to that which is good." This examination, says Luther, is not to be done by teachers. The teachers may only state what is to be examined. Judgment is given to the Christian people.[72] He sees Christ as positively taking the right and power to judge teaching from bishops, scholars, and councils and giving it to all Christians equally (John 10:4: "My sheep know my voice").[73] The same linking of judgment and "imposition" is noticeable in Thomas Rogers' account. He argues that the "Papists" maintain that "the pope of Rome hath the power to judge all men and matters, but may be judged of no man,"[74] that judgment goes with orders, "the power to judge of religion and points of doctrine is either in bishops only . . . or in their clergy only. . . ."[75] He himself contends with Luther that "authority is given to the Church, and to every member of sound judgment in the same, to judge in controversies of faith."[76]

We can, then, see in the sixteenth-century debates the beginnings of the realization of a number of implications about reception which have become clear only in our own century, but which were first thrown into the field of discussion by the shake-up of the foundational assumptions of ecclesiology on which Vincent of Lerins' dictum was based. Polemical considerations helped to shape the thinking of the day and made it difficult for the combatants to get away from the very analogy with human politics which was seen as a stumbling block by Melanchthon. The unique form of consensus which we call "reception" is peculiar to the Christian community. What, then, are the features of reception as they emerge in our own day in ecumenical discussion about Christian authority in matters of faith? Perhaps the salient features are exactly those to which the evidence we have been examining has been pointing us: It is a response, an active welcoming by the people of God. That is, it is not simply "the submission of obedience to a duly constituted authority," a "passive acquiescence,"[77] but both an intellectual consent ("an active exercise of the judgment") and a consent of the believing mind and heart,[78] in other words, it is a recognition. "By 'reception' we mean the fact that the people of God acknowledge . . . a decision or statement because they recognize in it the apostolic faith. They accept it because they discern a harmony between what is proposed to them and the *sensus fidelium* of the whole Church."[79] What is being recognized

91

is the voice of the Holy Spirit, "that through that definition, whether it was of a synod or a primate, the authentic, living voice of faith has been spoken in the Church, to the Church, by God."[80]

Because it is fundamentally an act of recognition, reception "does not create truth or legitimize the decision. It is the final indication that such a decision has fulfilled the necessary conditions for it to be a true expression of the faith."[81] But "our receiving has a positive, vital effect."[82] There is a living continuous process in tension with that which is eternal in Christian truth.

Chapter 7

TOWARD THE COMMON EXPRESSION OF THE APOSTOLIC FAITH TODAY: INTRODUCTION TO A FAITH AND ORDER PROJECT

Günther Gassmann

Introduction

It is highly appropriate that this Oxford Institute of Methodist Theological Studies integrate into its discussions on the identity and calling of the theological and spiritual heritage of Methodism the wider ecumenical search for rediscovering and expressing the common Christian identity and mission in this time of history. Indeed, no particular Christian tradition is any longer able to reflect, live, and act in isolation from the other ones. They are all called to transcend their own embodiment of the Christian faith by stretching out towards the universal dimension and significance of the Christian gospel encompassing all times, situations, and traditions. This universal dimension, in turn, becomes real and relevant in its concrete manifestations in specific cultural, socio-political and, I believe, also confessional/denominational contexts. There is thus a necessary interrelation between the particular and the universal, and this in more than a geographical sense.

This interrelation carries with it a great ecumenical potential. On the one hand, it can help to open up, enrich, and renew confessional traditions for the sake of their own identity and vitality, and it will at the same time contribute to their growing closer together on the way toward visible and effective forms of Christian unity. On the other hand, this interrelation can help to avoid a colorless "universal" or general Christianity which will be totally uninteresting to our contemporaries and which will have no chance of being taken seriously both in the intellectual debates and in the struggles and hopes of our time.

I am, therefore, grateful for the opportunity to introduce, together with my colleague Geoffrey Wainwright, a study project which offers ample room for testing and implementing the interrelation just indicated. The study project certainly needs the contribution of insights and experiences merging from the Methodist tradition. And the broad, universal scope of the project offers a framework which may assist Methodists in rediscovering and redefining their particular calling and mission as part of the wider ecumenical community.

The Study Project

At its meeting in January 1982 in Lima, Peru, the Commission on Faith and Order of the World Council of Churches (WCC) decided to launch a new study project under the title "Towards the Common Expression of the Apostolic Faith Today."[1] This title is not very precise. But even so it clearly indicates a new stage in the program of Faith and Order. After a period of thematic concentration on controversial issues, culminating in the adoption of the convergence document *Baptism, Eucharist and Ministry* at that same meeting at Lima, Faith and Order was now going to deal with the broader, comprehensive dimensions of the Christian faith. This decision was very much welcomed by the 1983 Vancouver Assembly of the WCC,[2] the Joint Working Group between the Roman Catholic Church and the WCC,[3] and many ecumenically concerned people and groups in the churches. Faith and Order is finally looking at the whole and not only at the parts—this seemed to be the impression undergirding these positive reactions.

By moving from the parts to the whole, however, one faces much more complex methodological problems than in dealing with narrower and limited issues. How can an international, interconfessional, intercultural theological community, which in itself carries all the potentials of mutual enrichment as well as conflict, cope with such a comprehensive theme which has been and still is interpreted in many different ways within Christianity? How can such a study process go beyond the limited circle of the Faith and Order Commission? And, most importantly, how can this process be shaped and oriented in such a way that there is realistic hope that the process itself and its results will contribute to the calling of the churches to common witness and confession in a divided world?

At the meeting of the Faith and Order Commission in Lima, such methodological and conceptual questions were already clarified to such a degree that the future course of the study on the apostolic faith seemed to be fairly obvious. The key element in this clarification was the decision to make the Creed of Nicea-Constantinople of 381 the starting point, focus, and goal of the study. On this basis three major elements and goals of the study were identified:

(a) A common *recognition* of the apostolic faith "as expressed in the Ecumenical Symbol of that faith: the Nicene Creed";

(b) A common *explication* of the apostolic faith" in the contemporary situations of the churches" by way of explicating the Nicene Creed for today;

(c) A common *confession* of the apostolic faith today on the basis of the Nicene Creed and its contemporary interpretation.[4]

The focus on the Nicene Creed was justified with the argument that it is the most widely accepted symbol of faith in both Western and Eastern Christianity, that it was in early church history an expression of the unity of the church, and that it has been received by many churches as an expression and summary of the fundamental articles of faith. These facts support the claim for the basic significance of this Creed for the ecumenical task of manifesting the unity of Christ's church.

However, the methodological and conceptual clarifications at Lima soon proved to be too optimistic and the ensuing study of the apostolic faith from 1984 until today has been constantly accompanied by a struggle with methodological questions. First of all, the strong focus on the Nicene Creed met with considerable reluctance and opposition from different sides. Because of their historical experience and theological conviction— the so-called "non-creedal churches"—or because of their historical, cultural, and social context — churches in the so-called third world—many churches have difficulties with fixed and authoritative formulas of faith in general and especially with those conceived in a distant period in the Mediterranean historical and cultural context. There was also the reminder that in many of the churches of the Christian West, the Apostles' Creed occupies a much more prominent role than the Nicene one. This led to serious doubts as to whether these experiences and convictions could be overcome simply by asking for a recognition of the Nicene Creed as a common ecumenical symbol and bond of unity. It was, therefore, soon decided to postpone work on this first element and goal— common recognition — of the Lima outline for the study.

Also the third element of the Lima outline, common confession of the apostolic faith today, soon proved anything but clear. It was obvious, and this was already affirmed at Lima, that the intention was not to formulate a new ecumenical creed. This was beyond the authority of the WCC and belonged properly only to a truly ecumenical council. Was the alternative the preparation of a document which could serve as a basis for common confession today? But how could such a document, given the unpredictable history in which we live, anticipate situations of challenge, crisis, and conflict which this common Christian witness and confession would call for? These and other questions are still with us.

The Standing Commission on Faith and Order responded in 1984 to this dilemma concerning the first and third element of the Lima outline by deciding to begin the study for focusing work on the second aspect of the outline, the common explication or interpretation of the apostolic faith for today.[5] Here we seemed to be on firmer ground. In 1984 and 1985 three international consultations—in India, France, and Zaire—produced first draft interpretations of the three articles of the Nicene Creed.[6] The steering group for this study revised the drafts and integrated them into one consistent document. The Plenary Commission on Faith and Order, at its meeting in 1985 at Stavanger, Norway, thoroughly discussed this document. Its criticism, comments and suggestions provided the basis for further revision. In 1986 and 1987 the steering group continued to work on the document by revising the existing text and adding new aspects. The study document "Confessing One Faith" is the sixth version of the text.[7] It has become the longest Faith and Order text so far (one hundred pages). In August 1987 it was presented to the Standing Commission on Faith and Order for final comments. Since then, it has been made available as a study document to churches, commissions and groups, seminars and individuals. This should encourage and enable broader participation in the task of explicating the apostolic faith for today. There seems to be a wide interest in this work—"Confessing One Faith" had to be reprinted twice—and several churches and ecumenical bodies have already begun to participate.

In the course of developing "Confessing One Faith" over the last three years, certain methodological and conceptual modifications became necessary. The explications of the three articles of faith start from the formulations of the Nicene Creed—without prejudging the issue of the recognition of this Creed. The Creed is used as an important summary which can help us focus our attention on fundamental convictions of the Christian faith. Each formula of the Creed, however, is directly related in the text to respective sections of the biblical witness which are foundational to these later formulations. This is to indicate that only by linking the Creed to the biblical witness and by interrelating the biblical witness and the early creeds does the term "apostolic faith" take on clearer contours.

But "apostolic faith" is not a historical concept in the sense of just looking back to the roots; that would be rather un-apostolic. Accordingly, the interpretation of the affirmations of the Nicene Creed in the context of their biblical basis is related to specific theological, religious, and social problems and challenges of our time and world. How can the belief in a Trinitarian God be interpreted in relation to the challenges coming from other monotheistic religions? The Creed as well as Christian faith and spirituality have followed Jesus in addressing God as "Father," but how can this be reinterpreted in a non-sexist way? What are the ethical consequences of the confession of God being the creator of all things, seen and unseen? How can we articulate the suffering and death of Jesus for us as a message of hope in a world full of suffering? What are the ecumenical convergences in relation to traditional controversial issues such as "filioque" or Mariology? In what way is eschatological hope becoming relevant for the struggles of humanity in present world history?

These are only some of the issues which are part of the contemporary horizon within which the fundamentals of faith are interpreted. This attempt is made in order to indicate in what way the affirmations of an ancient Creed can be actualized in new times and situations. It is also, and primarily so, in order to suggest common theological perspectives for a joint Christian witness in our world when and where such a witness is called for. Thus, the affirmations of the Creed are interpreted within the comprehensive framework of God's saving purpose and action in history from its beginning to its fulfillment. It is understandable that an effort with such a wide scope cannot be summarized in a relatively short document like the *BEM* text.

The Ecumenical Significance of the Study Project

The work on the explication of the apostolic faith on the basis of the Nicene Creed has been highly interesting and stimulating for those who have been involved in the process so far. Diverse concerns and priorities of people could come together because the biblical and historical material is combined in an attempt to interpret fundamental affirmations of the faith in the horizon of contemporary problems and challenges. We can expect similar experiences when the text is discussed in the churches, even though we have to underline that it is still a study document which will be further revised. We hope that by then we will have received quite a number of reactions from groups and individuals which can be fed into the discussions of the Commission. Only after several years will a more mature text be published and officially sent to the churches for their study and reaction. But interesting and stimulating as it may be, what is the ecumenical purpose of this enterprise of explicating the apostolic faith?

The oscillating term "apostolic faith" refers in the first instance to the content of the faith and not only to the obedient and confident act of faith in continuity with the apostles. Both aspects of the faith are, of course, deeply and inseparably interrelated. But if the term "apostolic faith" puts the emphasis on the content of faith, then the point of reference for faith so qualified is the apostolic witness which is normative for all times and places. It has this authority because it is the witness of the self-revelation of God in Jesus Christ. We receive this witness from witnesses empowered by the Holy Spirit: the disciples of Jesus; those whom the risen Christ sent out into all the world; the members of the first congregations who were enabled by the Holy Spirit to put all their trust and hope into the risen Lord.

The apostolic witness of all these people, going far beyond the inner circle of the twelve, is transmitted to us in the New Testament which, in its way, received the witness of the people of God in the Old Testament. This comprehensive apostolic witness was further clarified beyond the first generation with the help of structures of thinking and terminologies of that time. Such clarification was necessary because of conflicts with sectarian and heretical movements and because of the need to develop short formularies of faith for worship services, especially for baptismal confessions of faith. Such clarification in the form of creedal formulations was also required because of the necessity to arrive at some mutual understanding on the fundamental articles of faith as an expression of identity, and as a bond of unity for the Christian communities in view of the rapid expansion and diversification of Christianity. Thus, the creedal formulations of this early period are still to a certain extent part of that foundational apostolic witness, even though we have to make a distinction between them and the normative biblical witness. Apostolic faith then is the personal, corporate, and missionary witness and confession of faith in commitment to and continuity with the basic apostolic witness in holy scripture and in the early creeds.[8]

Such a rough, preliminary description of "apostolic faith" includes *per definitionem* an ecumenical and catholic dimension. When we say "apostolic faith" we are looking beyond our confessions and Christian traditions, despite our conviction that this apostolic faith receives historical expression, continuity, and lived faith in these same confessions and traditions. But we have also to realize that the fullness of this faith cannot be wholly comprehended and expressed by any one of our confessions and traditions. Could then the apostolic faith which is both in and beyond our churches, be or become the deepest bond which unites us despite our differences and divisions?

This ecumenical dimension is also present in the fact that all major Christian traditions emphatically affirm their commitment to the apostolic faith, notwithstanding their differences concerning the authority and role of the early creeds. Thus, if the apostolic faith is regarded as the authoritative witness of the saving action of the Triune God in creation, redemption, and fulfillment, then the communion, unity, and mission of those who live this faith must also be expressed in the common confession of this same faith. It is obvious, therefore, that the common confession of the apostolic faith should be the basis and starting point as well as the goal of ecumenical endeavors. It has to be the goal, because despite our commitment to our common roots, the Christian churches in their history have interpreted this apostolic faith in such diverse ways that they have become divided from each other.

This ecumenical dimension of the apostolic faith has been discovered rather late in ecumenical debate. In the early history of Faith and Order an attempt was made to introduce the early creeds as a bond of unity. This attempt was made under the influence of the Anglican Lambeth Quadrilateral, which made in its second point the acceptance of both the Apostles' and Nicene Creeds as a condition for reunion. This effort was, however, given up after the First World Conference on Faith and Order at Lausanne 1927 because of the different attitudes of the churches to creeds and confessions. Of course, basic elements of the apostolic faith have always been part of ecumenical discussion and statements, from the reflection on "Christ and the Church" at Lund 1952 (Third World Conference on Faith and Order) to "Baptism, Eucharist and Ministry." But they were always, as I said in the beginning, the parts—and usually the traditionally controversial parts—and never the whole of the apostolic faith.

This wholeness of the faith came more directly into view when the WCC began to formulate the goal of the unity we seek to manifest. When the famous "formula of unity" of the 1961 WCC Assembly at New Delhi enumerated the basic conditions and expressions of unity, it mentioned in the first place communion in "holding the one apostolic faith." Since then all descriptions of unity include the confession of, or the agreement in, the one apostolic faith as one of the basic requirements of unity. In 1975 the WCC Assembly at Nairobi asked the churches "to undertake a common effort to receive, reappropriate, and confess together, as contemporary occasion requires, the Christian truth and faith, delivered through the Apostles and handed down through the centuries."[9] This new emphasis on agreement in faith was taken up by the Faith and Order study on "Giving Account of the Hope that is in Us" (1971–1978)[10] and by the Joint Working Group between the Roman Catholic Church and the WCC in its reflections on "Towards a Confession of the Common Faith" (1978–1980).[11] Two Faith and Order consultations in 1978 and 1979 struggled with the "filioque" controversy,[12] and two further consultations in 1981 on the occasion of the 1500th anniversary of the Creed of Nicea-Constantinople highlighted the ecumenical significance of this Creed.[13] These and other developments reclaimed the ecumenical dimension of the apostolic faith and prepared the way for the decision at Lima 1982 to initiate the study process "Towards the Common Expression of the Apostolic Faith."

We have started this process, and we hope to broaden it beyond the limits of Faith and Order. There already seems to be a remarkable readiness and interest in many places to participate in this study. Just one example:

the Christian Council in Burma informed us that they have constituted a study group for this project. Also quite apart from this Faith and Order initiative we observe a number of projects in churches and worldwide Christian communions which point into similar directions. One possible explanation for this general tendency is the desire to reaffirm the foundations of Christian identity and communion in a world of increasing pluralism and religious choice. And with this goes the felt need to provide a deeper theological and spiritual basis for the faith and life of individual Christians and their churches. This is felt because they are more than ever before challenged to render their witness in words, deeds, and suffering by facing the complexities of our world, a world which has all the potentials of God's good creation which at the same time are being distorted in a way which threatens even the survival of humanity.

With this more general perspective we have not lost sight of the ecumenical dimension of the apostolic faith. On the contrary, it is exactly by turning again to our common apostolic roots in the perspective of our common mission that we are able to rediscover what we have in common, what unites us as Christians at the deepest level. It seems to be a favorable time for an ecumenical study on the apostolic faith even though we are also encountering here confessional differences and, perhaps even more, differences of theological positions and methodologies. This study has the potential of stimulating in churches and ecumenical bodies a reflection on the apostolic faith as an orientation for Christian life and witness today and at the same time the study can profit from the reflections that are already going on. It will then be the special responsibility and task of Faith and Order to bring together and formulate the insights of this shared process. At the end of this process there might hopefully come the moment when we will be able to say to and in the name of ecumenical Christianity: This is our common faith, founded on the witness of the apostles, reaffirmed, and reinterpreted for the church and the world at the end of the second millenium. This communion in the fundamentals of the faith is the deepest expression of the unity which already binds us together and which undergirds and inspires our unity in prayer, solidarity, and action. This communion provides us with the basis and the content for a common confession today wherever Christians are challenged to testify against the principalities and powers of this world and to incarnate God's love for those who cry out for life.

Chapter 8

METHODISM AND THE APOSTOLIC FAITH

Geoffrey Wainwright

It is tempting simply to declare that Methodism's best contribution to the World Council of Churches study on the Apostolic Faith would be to sit still and listen. But denominational honor requires that we participate more actively. The hope must be that the exercise will prove mutually beneficial to ourselves and to other participants.

The present chapter will correspondingly unfold in three stages. In the first part, we shall examine what Methodism might receive from the WCC Faith and Order project as it has been set up and is developing. In the second part, we shall suggest how Methodism might add to the project. In the third part, we shall try to discern more synthetically some possible results from the engagement in a common process.

In examining, in the first part, the Faith and Order program, we shall find the Apostolic Faith study to be marked by four characteristics that need to be restamped on contemporary Methodism. The study is: (a) creedal; (b) trinitarian; (c) ecumenical; (d) homological, that is, in the service of confessing the faith. These same four points will then also be used to structure Methodism's own potential contribution to the project (part two), and to discern some elements in a desired synthesis (part three).

In suggesting, in the second part, an authentic Methodist contribution to the project, we shall take as our paradigm John Wesley's "Letter to a Roman Catholic" of 1749. As is well known, this "olive branch," as Albert Outler calls it,[1] is not all that Wesley had to offer to the Romans: he could be polemical as well as irenical, as may be seen in "A Roman Catechism faithfully drawn out of the allowed writings of the Church of Rome, with a Reply thereto."[2] Nor is it claimed that Wesley was interested in relations with Roman Catholics to the exclusion of others. Our choice of paradigm depends on the fact that, in setting out "the faith of a true Protestant," Wesley proceeded by way of an expansion upon the Nicene-Constantinopolitan creed, the very procedure being followed in the Faith and Order study. The wider range of Wesley's ecumenical interests will be represented by our drawing also on his more generally intended sermon of 1750 on a "catholic spirit" (where the c is lower case).[3]

In the third, and more synthetic, part, we shall declare our desire that, in the give and take of study and the common pursuit, Methodism may be reconfirmed in a faith which is scriptural, patristic, Wesleyan, and (we hope) synchronically ecumenical. By its active and receptive participation in the Faith and Order project, Methodism may perhaps recover its Wesleyan heritage where we have abandoned it, reenter the catholic path where we have strayed from it, and maintain or restore Wesleyan impulses where the broader Christian Tradition needs them.

I. The Apostolic Faith Study

The current state of the WCC project "Towards the Common Expression of the Apostolic Faith Today" is represented in Faith and Order Paper No. 140, a study document which bears the title *"Confessing* One Faith: Towards an *Ecumenical* Explication of the Apostolic Faith as Expressed in the Nicene-Constantinopolitan *Creed* (381)."[4] The words I have underlined, coupled with the fact that the councils of Nicea and Constantinople settled precisely the *trinitarian* faith of the church, provide the four characteristics highlighted in our description. The project is, first, creedal.

1. Creedal

The Nicene-Constantinopolitan Creed (NC), not to the exclusion of the Apostles' Creed, is taken as "the theological basis and methodological tool for the explication of the apostolic faith."[5] The creed was chosen for these purposes after a lengthy debate involving such questions as: (a) Why not simply take the Scriptures? (b) Why fix on such an antique formulation as part of confessing the faith today? (c) Why be bound to a form that some have experienced as authoritarian? Answers were reached along the following lines respectively:

(a) The decision was taken in the conviction that this Creed represents "an exemplary and authentic summary of the apostolic faith"[6], "the same apostolic faith that was expressed in Holy Scriptures and summarized in the Creeds of the Early Church."[7] The councils of the fourth century would have preferred to stick entirely to scriptural language but needed to include a minimum of other terminology (e.g., the *homoousion*) in order to reject mistaken interpretations of the biblical witness. In any case, in the present project each phrase of NC has its "biblical foundation" carefully laid out.[8]

(b) "The decision was also taken in the recognition that the Nicene Creed served as an expression of unity of the early church and is, therefore, also of great importance for our contemporary quest for the unity of

Christ's Church."[9] The project is thus employing NC as part of the recognized ecumenical technique of getting back behind divisions to common ground, of rediscovering and reappropriating "common roots."[10] This procedure has enjoyed considerable success in the liturgical movement of our century and in such doctrinal convergences as are expressed in the Lima document on "Baptism, Eucharist and Ministry."[11]

(c) An anecdote may help. A Jamaican Baptist began by expressing all the suspicions which his cultural and denominational background would naturally lead him to entertain towards the "Greek metaphysical" vocabulary and "imperially oppressive" uses of NC; but he came to value its substantial affirmation of the deity and sovereignty of Christ over against theological liberalism.

As Methodists, we need to recover our creedal inheritance, and participation in the Faith and Order project can help us to do so. It is true that Wesley omitted Article VIII ("Of the Three Creeds") in his selection of the Anglican Articles for American Methodism (we know that he particularly disliked the damnatory clauses of the so-called Athanasian Creed), and that he removed NC in his abridgement of the Prayer Book communion order in *The Sunday Service*. He had, however, no quarrel with the substance of NC, as we shall see; and he retained the Apostles' Creed in his American service book. The "inheritance of the apostolic faith" and "the fundamental principles of the historic creeds" are part of the constitutional basis of the British Methodist Church. The Apostles' and Nicene Creeds figure in the current liturgical books of Methodism on both sides of the Atlantic and in many other parts of the world. We should make better use of them, both in the recitation of them, as a "performative act" of our faith, and in the evangelistic and catechetical tasks of *explicating* the faith (the need for which the WCC study fully recognizes).

2. Trinitarian

The Faith and Order project is necessarily trinitarian if it follows NC in substance and in structure. For the council of Nicea declared the Son of the Father to be "true God from true God," and the council of Constantinople proclaimed the sovereignty of the Holy Spirit who is worshiped and adored with the Father and the Son. And NC follows the threefold pattern common to creeds based on the baptismal interrogations that match the triune Name.

The tripartite structure of "Confessing One Faith" is in fact as follows:

I. We believe in one God

II. We believe in one Lord Jesus Christ

III. We believe in the Holy Spirit, the Church, and the life of the world to come.

Substantially, the text stresses the oneness of God, which is a unity of tripersonal communion, with the First Person as "the eternal source of that living trinitarian communion of love."[12] It is insisted that the Father is always the Father of the Son, and the Son is always the Son of the Father;[13] and the only Holy Spirit is "the Spirit [who] belongs to the eternal being of the Trinity" and is never "dissociated . . . from the work of Christ in the economy of God's salvation."[14]

The *doctrine* of the Trinity, as bound to the *reality* of the Trinity, is vital to our knowledge of God and to our salvation. As Athanasius and the Cappadocians argued at the various stages of the Arian controversy: only God can reveal God, only God can redeem, and only God can give participation in God. In our time and place, Methodists must not acquiesce in, let alone create, patterns of understanding, speech, and prayer that some are proposing in an effort to overcome "patriarchy" but which in fact threaten the Trinity.

Quite apart from the difficulty of principle in knowing whether one has lighted on a formulation just as good as, or now even preferable to, the divine Name used by Jesus and the writers of the New Testament, the alternatives or substitutes concretely proposed appear unsatisfactory in the light of the Christian doctrinal tradition. "Creator, Christ and Spirit" has an Arian ring; and, by reducing Christ and the Spirit to creatures, we should, as Athanasius and the Cappadocians argued, be undermining our salvation. "Creator, Redeemer, Sustainer" sounds Sabellian and is in any case purely functional, forfeiting the internal divine communion in which salvation gives us a share. Even at his most "catholic spirited," Wesley refused his hand to Arians, semi-Arians, Socinians, and Deists, for their heart was not right with his heart.[15]

A denomination which in practice allows baptisms to be performed under a divine name changed at the discretion of the minister or the candidate will, in the longer historical term and on the wider geographical scene, eventually bring all its baptisms into disrepute. This appears to be the danger in which the United Methodist Church in the United States finds itself at the moment.[16] Nor is it a matter of baptism alone, fundamental as that is. An isolated use of "Father, Son, and Holy Spirit" in baptism would lead to its becoming a petrified, or even a magical, formula. Father, Son and Holy Spirit need to be named as the story is told, as the word is preached, as candidates are baptized, as the congregation prays, as the eucharist is offered, as ministers are ordained, and as the people are blessed. As Methodists in America, we in particular need to regain the confidence to do that.

3. Ecumenical

The Faith and Order project also grounds its employment of NC in (a) widespread existing usage, and (b) the ecumenical aim:

(a) NC is "officially recognized and used by many churches within the ecumenical movement"; "the main content" of NC and the Apostles' Creed "is also present in the thinking and life of churches which do not explicitly recognize these Creeds or use them in their teaching and worship."[17] Here again the study is following a familiar principle in ecumenical work, this time that of building on what the churches already have in common. The need now is for what is called, in an ungainly expression, the "re-reception" of the ancient creeds. For that reason, the *explication* of the creeds is important, even internally to the Christian community, let alone vis-a-vis the world (a point to which I shall return).

(b) The aim of the Faith and Order project is ecumenical in the classical sense of the ecumenical movement. "It serves the primary function and purpose of the WCC 'to call the churches to the goal of visible unity in one faith and in one eucharistic fellowship' [*Constitution of the WCC*, III.1]. The common confession of the apostolic faith is one of the essential conditions and elements of visible unity."[18]

As Methodists we should not jettison what we already hold in common with other Christians, either for the sake of emphasizing a "specific difference" or for the sake of a new will-o'-the-wisp that might bring us closer to other revisionists while severing the ties that bind us to the continuing historic Tradition. Rather we should find our strength in unity with others who hold fast to common Christianity.

As Methodists, again, we need to recommit ourselves to the goal of unity, "visible unity" as the 1986 Nairobi Report of the Joint Commission between the World Methodist Council and the Roman Catholic Church puts it; and to the search for appropriate models and means to realize that unity. In the 1970s and 1980s, British Methodists were frustrated by failures in the plans for reunion with the Church of England and for a covenant with other churches in England; American Methodists show little enthusiasm for the various proposals that have emerged from the Consultation on Church Union (COCU). What lessons, positive and negative, are to be drawn from Methodist participation in the United Church of Canada, the Church of South India, the Uniting Church in Australia? How are we to respect both the truly local and the truly universal dimensions of the unity to which the church is called? In any case, agreement "in the faith" is required for visible unity; and NC, as a common global text for common particular explication, appears to provide the best hope for progress in that direction.

4. Homological

In the title of the Faith and Order project, the broader term "common *expression*" is employed, but the elemental form of expression is the *confession* of the faith. Common confession of the faith is needed for united worship, life and mission. Made both *coram Deo* and *coram hominibus*, confession is at once (a) doxological, (b) evangelistic, and (c) ethical, in intention and scope. The Faith and Order document brings this out:

(a) The commentary to I/10 speaks of "the mystery of the triune God celebrated in the liturgy of the Church." Under pneumatology and ecclesiology, the doxological vision is extended to what the Orthodox have taken to calling "the liturgy after the Liturgy":

Christians, therefore, glorify the triune God through prayer, common worship and *the daily service which is their acceptable sacrifice* (cf. Rom. 12:1f.).[19]

The Church is the eucharistic community . . . whose basic calling is the glorification of the triune God in worship and service.[20]

(b) The WCC study shows a strong awareness that the apostolic faith expressed in NC has to be "explicated" in relation to the "challenges"— perennial and contemporary—that it faces. In appropriate circumstances, evangelism may be served either by direct proclamation of the gospel, or by apologetic, or by learning from outside critiques.

(c) The explication exemplified in Faith and Order Paper 140 also relates "doctrinal affirmations to ethical problems."[21] Thus the project is linked to other ecumenical concerns for peace, justice, and the integrity of creation.

As Methodists, we need to recover the Wesleyan fusion of confession *coram Deo* and *coram hominibus*. One of the most remarkable features of the Wesleyan revival was in fact the combination of hymnography, eucharistic observance, evangelistic preaching, changed lives, and charitable action.

II. The Wesleyan Paradigm

Apart from a few ill-formulated sentences scattered in his writings, Wesley did not minimize orthodoxy of belief. When he writes, for instance, that "orthodoxy, or right opinions, is at best a slender part of religion, if it can be allowed to be any part at all,"[22] it must be remembered, first, that Wesley was prepared to "think and let think" only in those matters of theological "opinion" that did not "strike at the root of Christianity;"[23] and second, that orthodoxy in the stricter sense of doctrine was, for Wesley, not so much unnecessary as insufficient—if it was not believed, experienced, and lived.

1. Creedal

Attention to Wesley could help the Faith and Order project to keep together "the faith which is believed" and "the faith which believes," the *fides quae creditur* and the *fides qua creditur*. Wesley's "Letter to a Roman Catholic" (*LRC*) first sets out the *content* of "the faith of a true Protestant," and then goes on to the *attitude, act,* and *conduct* of faith.[24]

That Wesley's substantive statement of faith is based on NC, rather than the Apostles' Creed alone, receives confirmation at several points:

- The fuller form of "*one* God, the Father,the Almighty, maker of heaven and earth, *of all things visible and invisible*" appears to provide more ground for Wesley's "I believe that this one God is the Father of all things, especially of angels and men"; and it may even be that the Greek παντοκρατόρα, rather than the Latin *omnipotentem*, stands behind Wesley's ensuing "I believe this Father of all not only to be able to do whatsoever pleaseth him but also to have an eternal right of making what and when and how he pleaseth; and of possessing and disposing of all that he has made; and that he of his own goodness created heaven and earth, and all that is therein."[25]

- The Nicene phrases concerning the eternity and consubstantiality of the Son are repeated in Wesley's "the Father of his only Son, whom he hath begotten from eternity,"[26] "the proper, natural Son of God, God of God, very God of very God."[27]

- The Nicene "who for us human beings and for our salvation" is expanded by Wesley's reference to the threefold office, prophet, priest and king, of "the Saviour of the world."[28]

- The Nicene σαρκόθεντα is given Chalcedonian precision by Wesley's "I believe that he was made man, joining the human nature with the divine in one person, being conceived by the singular operation of the Holy Ghost and born of the Blessed Virgin Mary."[29]

- When Wesley explicitly makes the Spirit "equal with the Father and the Son,"[30] he is benefiting from the council of Constantinople.

Then Wesley describes the *fides qua creditur* in this way:

A true Protestant believes in God, has a full confidence in his mercy, fears him with a filial fear, and loves him with all his soul. He worships God in spirit and in truth, in everything gives him thanks, calls upon him with his heart as well as his lips, at all times and in all places, honours his holy Name and his Word, and serves him truly all the days of his life.[31]

The integration of the *fides quae creditur* and the *fides qua creditur* is even more clearly and powerfully expressed in the sermon on "Catholic Spirit," when he sets out in section I what he means by the question "Is thine heart right, as my heart is with thy heart?"[32]

12. Is thy heart right with God? Dost thou believe his being and his perfections, his eternity, immensity, wisdom, power, his justice, mercy and truth? Dost thou believe that he now "upholdeth all things by the word of his power" [Heb. 1:3],and that he governs even the most minute, even the most noxious, to his own glory and the good of them that love him [cf. Rom. 8:28]? Hast thou a divine evidence, a supernatural conviction, of the things of God [cf. Heb. 11:1]? Dost thou "walk by faith, not by sight," looking not at temporal things but things eternal [2 Cor. 5:7; cf. 4:18]?

13. Dost thou believe in the Lord Jesus Christ, "God over all, blessed for ever" [Rom. 9:5]? Is he revealed in thy soul [cf. Gal. 1:15]? Dost thou "know Jesus Christ and him crucified" [1 Cor. 2:2]? Does he "dwell in thee and thou in him" [1 John 4:13, 15]? Is he "formed in thy heart by faith" [Gal. 4:19; cf. Eph. 3:17]? Having absolutely disclaimed all thy own works, thy own righteousness, hast thou "submitted thyself unto the righteousness of God" [Rom. 10:3], which is by faith in Christ Jesus? Art thou "found in him, not having thy own righteousness, but the righteousness which is by faith" [Phil. 3:9]? And art thou, through him, "fighting the good fight of faith, and laying hold of eternal life" [1 Tim. 6:12]?

14. Is thy faith ἐνεργουμένη δι' ἀγάπης, "filled with the energy of love" [Gal. 5:6]? Dost thou love God—I do not say "above all things," for it is both an unscriptural and ambiguous expression, but—"with all thy heart, and with all thy mind, and with all thy soul, and with all thy strength" [Luke 10:27]? Dost thou seek all thy happiness in him alone? And dost thou find what thou seekest [cf. Matt. 7:8]? Does thy soul continually "magnify the Lord, and thy spirit rejoice in God thy Saviour" [Luke 1:46f.]? Having learned "in everything to give thanks" [1 Thess. 5:18], dost thou find "it is a joyful and pleasant thing to be thankful" [Ps. 147:1]? Is God the centre of thy soul, the sum of all thy desires? Art thou accordingly "laying up" thy "treasure in heaven" [Matt. 6:20] and "counting all things else dung" and dross [Phil. 3:8]? Hath the love of God cast the love of the world out of thy soul? Then thou art "crucified to the world" [Gal. 6:14]; thou art dead to all below and thy "life is hid with Christ in God" [Col. 3:3].[33]

The trinitarian structure of these three paragraphs is clear, particularly when it is remembered, in connection with paragraph 14, that "the love of God is shed abroad in our hearts *by the Holy Spirit*" (Rom. 5:5). Wesley then continues in similar vein with questions concerning the service of God, love of neighbor, and good works.[34]

2. Trinitarian

Wesley refused to speculate on *how*, while firmly believing *that* Father, Son, and Holy Spirit are one God. Although he sometimes hesitated to impose the terms "person" and "Trinity" (apparently on account of their not being directly scriptural), he knew that the game would be lost with a surrender to mere functionalism: "The quaint device of styling them three offices rather than persons," he wrote to Jane Catherine March on August 3, 1771, "gives up the whole doctrine."[35] Wesley knew that the divine work in the world, the experience of believers, and the final kingdom all found their basis and implicate in the ontological reality of "the Three-One God."

Wesley's trinitarian preaching carries a strong soteriological interest. Listen to a sermon of 1775 directly "On the Trinity," in which he shows how "knowledge of the Three-One God is interwoven with all true Christian faith, with all vital religion":

> I know not how anyone can be a Christian believer till "he hath" (as St. John speaks) "the witness in himself"; till "the Spirit of God witnesses with his spirit that he is a child of God"—that is, in effect, till God the Holy Ghost witnesses that God the Father has accepted him through the merits of God the Son—and having this witness he honours the Son and the blessed Spirit "even as he honours the Father." Not every Christian believer *adverts* to this; perhaps at first not one in twenty; but if you ask any of them a few questions you will easily find it is implied in what he believes.[36]

And again, in the final salvation envisioned in a sermon of 1785 on "The New Creation":

> And to crown all, there will be a deep, an intimate, an uninterrupted union with God; a constant communion with the Father and his Son Jesus Christ, through the Spirit; a continual enjoyment of the Three-One God, and of all the creatures in him.[37]

In Wesley's "Letter to a Roman Catholic," this soteriological dimension of the doctrine and reality of the Trinity comes to the fore already in the exposition of the first article of NC:

> I believe that this one God ... is in a peculiar manner the Father of those whom he regenerates by his Spirit, whom he adopts in his Son as coheirs with him and crowns with an eternal inheritance.[38]

The insertion of the *munus triplex* in the second article has already been referred to:

> I believe that Jesus of Nazareth was the Saviour of the world, the Messiah so long foretold; that, being anointed with the Holy Ghost, he was a *prophet*, revealing to us the whole will of God; that he was a *priest*, who gave himself a sacrifice for sin, and still makes intercession for transgressors; that he is a *king*,

who has all power in heaven and in earth, and will reign till he has subdued all things to himself.[39]

Christ's sovereignty is likewise presented soteriologically:

I believe . . . that he is Lord of all, having absolute, supreme, universal dominion over all things; but more particularly *our* Lord (who believe in him), both by conquest, purchase, and voluntary obligation.[40]

The soteriological orientation of Wesley's confession concerning the Holy Spirit will appear in a moment.

In Faith and Order Paper 140, the soteriological orientation of the exposition of the second article emerges clearly from the titles of the sections on the Son:

A. Jesus Christ, incarnate for our salvation
B. Jesus Christ, suffering and crucified for us
C. Jesus Christ, risen to overcome evil powers.

Perhaps the explication concerning the Holy Spirit could be clearer in its soteriology, not only in the paragraph headings but in the substantive connections made between the divine ontology and human salvation. True, the ecclesiological section includes a paragraph on the church as "communion of saints in the Spirit." But many Evangelicals, and not they alone, would be helped by a corresponding emphasis on the direct work of the Holy Spirit in the heart and lives of believers. Wesley shows the way in *LRC*:

I believe the infinite and eternal Spirit of God, equal with the Father and the Son, to be not only perfectly holy in himself, but the immediate cause of all holiness in us: enlightening our understandings, rectifying our wills and affections, renewing our natures, uniting our persons to Christ, assuring us of the adopted of sons, leading us in our actions, purifying and sanctifying our souls and bodies to a full and eternal enjoyment of God.[41]

3. Ecumenical

Wesley's *LRC* can set an example for the conduct of the Faith and Order dialogue in at least three ways:

(a) The *human, and Christian, respect and concern* which are shown towards one's conversation partners. Wesley considered the Roman Catholic Church to be in doctrinal error on a number of important points; but he could at times regard it as at least *part* of the church catholic, and certainly he recognized individual Roman Catholics as Christian. In *LRC* Wesley grounds his regard for his interlocutor not only in the universally creative and redemptive work of God but also in the Christian intention of serious Roman Catholics:

I think you deserve the tenderest regard I can show, were it only because the same God hath raised you and me from the dust of the earth and has made us both capable of loving and enjoying him to eternity; were it only because the Son of God has bought you and me with his own blood. How much more, if you are a person fearing God (as without question many of you are) and studying to have a conscience void of offence towards God and towards man?[42]

The partners ought at the least never to hurt one another deliberately, either in deed, word, or thought:

In the name, then, and in the strength of God, let us resolve first, not to hurt one another, to do nothing unkind or unfriendly to each other, nothing which we would not have done to ourselves. Rather let us endeavour after every instance of a kind, friendly and Christian behaviour towards each other.

Let us resolve, secondly, God being our helper, to speak nothing harsh or unkind of each other. The sure way to avoid this is to say all the good we can, both of and to one another; in all our conversation, either with or concerning each other, to use only the language of love. . . .

Let us, thirdly, resolve to harbour no unkind thought, no unfriendly temper towards each other. Let us lay the axe to the root of the tree, let us examine all that rises in our heart and suffer no disposition there which is contrary to tender affection.[43]

More positively yet:

If God still loveth us, we ought also to love one another. We ought . . . to provoke one another to love and to good works.[44]

The goal is eschatological:

Let us . . . endeavour to help each other on in whatever we are agreed leads to the kingdom.[45]

I hope to see *you* in heaven.[46]

(b) Wesley sets *a methodological and hermeneutical principle* by his distinction between vital "doctrines," on the one hand, and the "opinions" on which theological schools may differ as long as they do so on the same basis of faith. "I say not a word to you about your opinions," writes Wesley to the Roman Catholic[47] and calls for a stop to the "endless jangling about opinions."[48] True, the distinction between doctrine and opinion is not always easy to make; but all Christian traditions do in fact make such distinctions *within* their own fellowship (e.g., Molinists vs. Thomists within the Roman Catholic Church), and there is no reason why the propriety and inevitability of making such distinctions should not be recognized *across* confessional boundaries from the very start of the search for agreement in the faith.

Similarly, Wesley allows variety in "outward manner of worship" in a way which would allow diversity of "rites" within a single communion:

> Be your form of worship what it will, but in every thing give him thanks; else it is all but lost labour. Use whatever outward observances you please, but put your whole trust in him, but honour his holy Name and his Word, and serve him truly all the days of your life.[49]

Again, it is not always easy to draw the limits of possible and welcome variety within a worship that is to remain solidly scriptural and trinitarian; but distinctions of the kind that were made between doctrine and opinion with respect to the "lex credendi" are surely allowable between, say, a sacrament and the ceremonial manner of its observance in the "lex orandi."

(c) There is the matter of *openness to other traditions*. Wesley was prepared to make what may at first blush appear to be "accommodations," even in matters of significant doctrine and practice; but it could well turn out that Wesley was bringing forward in dialogue with the Roman Catholic certain items that had not entirely disappeared from Protestantism, and whose recovery might even now help Methodism's settlement in the catholic tradition in both East and West. Thus he confesses Christ to be "born of the Blessed Virgin Mary, who, as well after as before she brought him forth, continued a pure and unspotted virgin."[50] And he believes that Christians "have fellowship with the holy angels who constantly minister to these heirs of salvation, and with all the living members of Christ on earth, as well as all who are departed this life in his faith and fear."[51] Participants in the Faith and Order study on the Apostolic Faith should be willing to open themselves to treasures that have been better preserved, insights that have been more vitally lived, in other parts of the great Christian Tradition than their own.

4. Homological

Wesley's *LRC* instantiates the same three aspects of confessing the faith as we noted in Faith and Order Paper 140: (a) doxological; (b) evangelistic; (c) ethical. Wesley's example and exhortations concerning process and goal could be heeded by all participants in the WCC project:

(a) with regard to glorifying God:

> All worship is an abomination to the Lord unless you worship him in spirit and in truth, with your heart as well as your lips, with your spirit and your understanding also.[52]

> Do you do all as unto the Lord, as a sacrifice unto God, acceptable in Christ Jesus?[53]

(b) All Wesley's evangelistic activity is set under the initiative of the *missio Dei* and the free grace of God, as confessed by Wesley to the Roman Catholic:

> I believe that Christ and his Apostles gathered unto himself a church to which he has continually added such as shall be saved. . . .[54]

> I believe that God forgives all the sins of them that truly repent and unfeignedly believe his holy gospel. . . .[55]

Evangelism was not directly Wesley's theme in writing to the Roman Catholic, but it is interesting for Faith and Order purposes that his language in the Letter may at times reflect an awareness of contemporary philosophico-theological controversies, if not an apologetic intent. In the century of the Enlightenment, he precedes his credo with a subordinate clause: "As I am assured that there is an infinite and independent Being and that it is impossible that there should be more than one, so I believe that this one God is [the Holy Trinity]."[56] The same issues live on in the efforts of Faith and Order Paper 140 to situate the God confessed by Christians in relation to Judaism, to Islam, to the religious search of humankind, to idolatry, and to atheism.[57]

(c) Wesley writes that "a true Protestant loves his neighbour (that is, every man, friend or enemy, good or bad) as himself, as he loves himself, as he loves his own soul, as Christ loved us. And as Christ laid down his life for us, so he is ready to lay down his life for his brethren."[58] It is important that the WCC, in its battle against systemic evil, should not neglect to address the sanctification of the believer as part of Christian witness. If the dimension of personal conduct finds little place in the present study, many Evangelicals, and not they alone, will find it difficult to recognize the description of the apostolic faith.

III. Hopes For Unity

We saw, first, some needs of contemporary Methodism, which participation in the Apostolic Faith project might help to meet. We offered, second, a Wesleyan paradigm which might both encourage Methodist participation in the Faith and Order study and provide substantive and procedural help for the whole project. In this third part, it is now time to express more synthetically some further hopes concerning the results of the Faith and Order exercise for both Methodism and the church universal.

1. Creedal

The focus on the creeds allows an understanding and practice of the relation between Scripture and Tradition in ways that were convergently expressed by the Fourth World Conference on Faith and Order at Montreal in 1963 and the near-simultaneous Vatican II text on "Divine Revelation" (*Dei Verbum*). Scripture was there understood as the internal norm of Tradition, and Tradition as the immediate interpretative context of Scripture. Now, the traditional creeds are grounded in the same apostolic faith as comes to expression in the Scriptures:

- they provide a summary of the biblical story of creation, redemption, and consummation;
- they clarify the implied ontological basis of the story in the reality of God;
- they engage the believing church in the transmission of the story and the reality through reception and proclamation.

Thus the creeds and the study of them provide both content and methodological model for all controversial questions where the relation of Scripture and Tradition is at stake.

Participation in the present project should help all partners to understand better (certainly some Methodist responses show a lack in this regard) the procedures that were followed in producing the Lima text on *Baptism, Eucharist and Ministry*, and perhaps to improve on the results achieved in the Lima document. The kind of interplay between Scripture and Tradition represented by the Apostolic Faith study should prove fundamentally congenial to Methodists. That Wesley was "a man of one book" (*homo unius libri*), namely the Scriptures, does not indicate a "boundary of his reading" so much as "the center of gravity in his thinking."[59] He sought thereby to live in the continuing Tradition of the apostolic faith. The creedal basis and method of the Faith and Order project should allow the churches to grow together into a commonly accepted understanding and practice of Scripture and Tradition.

2. Trinitarian

The trinitarian shape and content of the WCC project brings us to the most vital point of action at the level of fundamental faith. The signs are that the doctrine of the Trinity is becoming once again, as it was in the fourth century, the *articulus stantis et cadentis ecclesiae*. For the doctrine expresses who the God is, who is the source, sustenance and goal of the redemption of humankind. At stake is the identity of God, and the nature of God's presence and action in the world.

To take only one case: Western liberal Christianity, or in U.S. terms the "mainline churches," are for various reasons in danger of losing their grasp on the understanding and practice of the Triune God. Evidence can be found in recent liturgical compositions. The 1986 *Book of Worship* of the

United Church of Christ practically limits the use of the scriptural and traditional name of Father, Son and Holy Spirit to baptism. The successive revisions leading to the United Methodist *Book of Services* (1985) manifest an increasingly feeble grasp of the Trinity (although, happily, the 1989 *Hymnal* fares better). The same is true of the "Supplemental Liturgical Resources" in the Presbyterian Church in the U.S.A. (although, as an invited advisor, I was able to restore a few modest trinitarian references in the eucharistic prayers for *The Service for the Lord's Day* of 1984).

To touch on the most neuralgic point: the Faith and Order text, while sensitive to the motherly as well as the fatherly aspects of God's care for us, roundly declares:

> In Jesus' language about God, "Father" is not only an image, it is primarily the *name* of the God to whom he relates in his mission and whose kingdom he proclaims. It is the name used to address God in prayer. In its function as a name, the name of God in Jesus' own teaching and prayer, the word "Father" cannot be replaced by another one. It would no longer be the God of Jesus to whom we relate if we were to exclude the name Jesus himself used.[60]

Deeper reflection in the context of the ecumenical study might help the truly liberating character of God to emerge from the overlay of obfuscating and oppressive practices of "patriarchalism":

> Paul indicates that God is our Father because he is first the Father of Jesus, who graciously allows us to share by adoption in that unique Father-Son relationship. Furthermore, it is the Spirit who unites us with the Son and who sets us free as his sisters and brothers, to call God "Abba." What Paul says of "sons" he says also of daughters (2 Cor. 6:16–18): communion with the Father is open to all human beings without differentiation (cf. Rom. 8:14–15; Gal. 4:6).[61]

This, again, should be congenial to Methodists. For Wesley, "adoption" was a major soteriological category. To call God "Abba, Father" was the privilege of believers, not an alien imposition. One of the Wesleys' greatest hymns, dating from the *Hymns and Sacred Poems* of 1739, runs as follows:

Since the Son hath made me free,
Let me taste my liberty;
Thee behold with open face,
Triumph in thy saving grace,
Thy great will delight to prove,
Glory in thy perfect love.

115

Abba, Father, hear thy child,
Late in Jesus reconciled;
Hear, and all the graces shower,
All the joy, and peace, and power,
All my Saviour asks above,
All the life and heaven of love.

Heavenly Adam, Life divine,
Change my nature into thine;
Move and spread throughout my soul,
Actuate and fill the whole;
Be it I no longer now
Living in the flesh, but thou.

Holy Ghost, no more delay;
Come, and in thy temple stay;
Now thine inward witness bear,
Strong, and permanent, and clear;
Spring of life, thyself impart,
Rise eternal in my heart.

3. Ecumenical

The Apostolic Faith study sets the wider dogmatic context for particular doctrinal discussions in Faith and Order—a context whose inescapability was in fact recognized as early as the First World Conference on Faith and Order at Lausanne in 1927. Renewed attention to the full scope of Christian belief, as expressed in the creeds, would "correct" what some, including some Methodists, have felt to be the "narrow" sacramentalism of *Baptism, Eucharist and Ministry*. (Carefully read, *BEM* covers a wider dogmatic range, since the sacraments themselves are there shown to have— as, say, the Wesleys' *Hymns on the Lord's Supper* make clear—trinitarian, christological, ecclesiological and eschatological reference.)

The Apostolic Faith study is valuable, too, in so far as it provides the multilateral context needed to keep all the churches honest in their respective bilateral dialogues. It should prevent them from saying contradictory things to and with different partners. This is an important consideration for the World Methodist Council in its various dialogues with the Roman Catholics, the Lutherans, and the Reformed.

Finally, the Apostolic Faith study should help all churches together to rediscover what Wesley understood by the *analogia fidei*, the "proportion of the faith":—the place and connection of the main elements of belief within a range of patterns that are recognizably ecumenical in time and space.

4. Homological

By combining the doxological, kerygmatic and ethical components in the confession of faith, the WCC project should help to hold together the varying dominant interests of particular groups within Methodism and across the confessional board: the liturgical, the evangelistic, and the social-activist. This is vital to the integrity of a denominational tradition that looks to Wesley, and to the rounded prosecution of its calling by the whole church universal. We need to ensure that it is the *same faith* which is being confessed in the *various modes* of worship, mission and service.

Last of all, the gathering of Christians from the four winds around the theme of the Apostolic Faith should facilitate that proclamation and embodiment of the *one gospel* in *diverse cultural circumstances* which have been the aim of Christianity, and of Methodism, since their beginnings.

Chapter 9

PLURALISM: THE RELATIONSHIP OF THEOLOGY TO RELIGIOUS STUDIES

Adrian Hastings

Pluralism is, I believe, a matter of absolutely primary importance for theologians, philosophers, students of religion, and human beings, because human and religious experience is irremediably pluralist. But pluralism has come to have so many forms and meanings which require to be distinguished rather carefully if their consideration is not to become hopelessly confused. My intention in this paper is to consider one quite limited, almost methodological, aspect of the subject by focusing on two rather closely linked developments within the recent intellectual history of the Christian West: one, the transformation of university departments of "theology" into departments of "religious studies" (either by change of name or effectively); the other, the proposed transformation of Christian theology itself, with its hitherto irreducible core of particularism, into a pluralist "world theology" which gives no centrality or primacy to any specific religious tradition of revelation or salvation. The latter is, of course, particularly connected with names like John Hick and Wilfred Cantwell Smith. These two developments have gone very closely together, the one often appearing as the justification of the other. They might well be claimed to represent collectively the most characteristic contribution of the late 1960s and 70s to the theological area of study.

I will begin with what might be called, a little simplistically, an attempt to delineate the *Sitz im Leben* of John Hick's *God and the Universe of Faiths*.[1] The establishment of a *Sitz im Leben*, as should be obvious (but it often is not), in no way demonstrates the truth or falsity of an idea, but understanding is undoubtedly helped by the contextualization of its genesis. The book was published in 1973 and represents the most influential example in this country of the rewriting of Christian theology to accommodate the apparent requirements of a religiously pluralistic world. It is of course closely paralleled by the work of Wilfred Cantwell Smith[2] in America, among others. To understand this exercise, and the apparent need for it, it seems to me helpful to consider the cultural world which had finally broken up a few years previously. It was not, strange as it may seem in retrospect, a pluralistic world. It is true that beginning with the seventeenth century, at least, the West was laying the intellectual and religious foundations for pluralism. It is true also that for two hundred years the British Empire had straddled cultures and faiths with, on the whole, remarkable tolerance and aplomb: India could not have been ruled otherwise. But it was only, and very deliberately, tolerance up to a point. Indian culture and religion, it was officially agreed, were good enough for Indians, but they were not something fully open to an Englishman—however affectionate a Kipling or a Forster, at least, might be towards them. The underlying tragedy of *A Passage to India* lies precisely therein. Indian culture and society could be a tourist attraction, but it would be very dangerous for all concerned if they became more than that.

The Victorian model coupled a worldwide empire and commerce with the most emphatic commitment, explicit or implicit, to the mental, moral, and religious primacy of Western man, conceived in a unitary and rather missionary way. Despite the growth of a multiplicity of denominations, a pluralism of public experience was not significantly reflected in a pluralism of world view but rather in an unquestioning consciousness of superiority, guaranteed by printing press and gun, railroad and telegraph. Perhaps there was no other way in which Europe's political domination could have been appropriately justified or motivated. If a diversity of culture and religion was all the same admitted, it was then not on a fully pluralistic basis but on a strictly two tier model: ours and theirs, and never the twain shall meet.

Ours was not as such necessarily Christian—or at least it did not remain so. Take that much-used nineteenth century phrase "civilization and Christianity." For some people the one took primacy, for some the other. The missionary, expatiating upon the power and wealth of Queen Victoria's empire to a bemused petty African potentate, might wave the Bible before him and declare impressively, "Here is the explanation of Britain's greatness," but the late Victorian mind was increasingly regarding the Christianity element in the package as expendable, and for some colonial officials it was just a nuisance. One remained no less firmly convinced of the inherent superiority of Westernness.

Certainly the typical missionary, lay theologian, or person in the pew rather easily equated the most particularist claims of Christianity, of Christ, of Bible, the *"solus"* of Reformation theology, with the inner principle of the West's primacy, the conclusive reason why Britain was *super omnes*. England's providential role, declared Frederick Temple, at the time a young man, but later to be Archbishop of Canterbury, was "the sublimest position ever occupied by any nation hitherto, that of the authoritative propagator of the Gospel over the world."[3] The theological and religious particularism always inherent in the Christian gospel took on or coalesced with, in the context of the nineteenth century, this world-embracing Western cultural particularism of political, even racial, domination—a domination which would not exterminate other breeds and faiths, but regulate them, study them conscientiously, hopefully perhaps in due course convert them. *Christus vincit* melted into "Britannia rules the waves" and the more confident one was in the inherent superiority of Victoria's Britain, the more affected one might be both with a high sense of protectionist duty towards lesser breeds and by the call of the student Christian's new watch-word "The evangelization of the world in this generation."[4]

Of course I am simplifying, even perhaps caricaturing a little, the world view of our ancestors—the world view in which at least some of us were still brought up. But not too greatly. In the first half of the twentieth century it was expressed less crudely and less confidently, yet it survived and, indeed, a large working empire continued to require it as a sort of civil religion. The final collapse of this civil religion came only after the Second World War and even then not too quickly. But the conditions which both needed and stimulated it were rapidly disappearing. The economic and political decline of Britain in particular was obvious. By the mid-1960s the Empire had virtually disappeared. The United Nations had generated a new ethos of egalitarian international relations. Japan, China, Indonesia, India, and Pakistan were major powers. Christianity had lost such worldwide political significance as it possessed prior to the 1939–45 war. Even within Europe the struggle between religion and secular humanism which had continued within the Western tradition for many generations seemed to have reached a new phase in the ever more apparent triumph of the latter.

The 1960s were the decade in which the customary ideology of the West became manifestly unnecessary and hence patently absurd. It happened coincidentally, but perhaps not wholly coincidentally, with other, less easily to be anticipated, cultural revolutions: a general deriding of structure and tradition, a discovery of permissiveness, community, and experience: culture-free, gender-free, race-free.[5] The quintessential qualities of the sixties seemed everything that the Victorian spirit was not. This transformation, partially but by no means wholly ephemeral, was made a great deal more complex for Britain by an extra but not unrelated development—the arrival of hundreds of thousands of Caribbean and Asian immigrants, the latter bringing their own non-Christian religions. Britain itself was becoming religiously a highly pluralistic society in which Muslim, Sikh, Hindu, and Buddhist communities were important, just at the time when its Christian commitment was, at least in numerical terms, declining more rapidly than in any previous decade of the century, and just, too, as the old model of a two-tiered humanity was disappearing as absurd.

Western people had lived hitherto — even, paradoxically, if they lived in India or Malaysia—in an essentially unpluralistic society and that society was motivated by an unpluralistic Western religion, whether Christian or liberal humanist, the two accommodatingly interwoven. All that was now over. In the sixties our Western world became stridently pluralist. The model was no longer Eton but California. Strangely enough, just as the traditionally unitary and missionary West turned in aspiration pluralist and undogmatic, much of the rest of the world began to move with almost equal suddenness and even cruelty towards unitary, anti-pluralist models. The late 1960s can be seen as a crucial moment for both developments. So much so, in fact, that Western society's rather hastily embraced pluralist ideals, intended especially to accommodate the religions of Asia, could create new grounds for suspicion for others rather than any obvious bridge. It is within an almost worldwide anti-pluralist surge that the modern Western concern for pluralism must be assessed.

In the late 1960s, however, that was not evident and the newly perceived cultural pluralism of the West could well be seen as standing in need of a civil religion grounded in an appropriate theology. No faith should be established, yet each should be accorded appropriate respect and drawn into the functions that society asks of civil religion. There was an implicit need of an intellectual framework for the new religious order, even if that order could not fully be brought into being all at once. The interrelationship of religions could, of course, be looked at in purely secular sociological or historical terms, even in Marxist ones, but to a religious sympathizer such terms would be reductionist and demeaning. Civil religion and the theology behind it must not be that. Parallel approaches to a number of different religious traditions must inevitably generate institutions which are in principle religiously pluralist—that is to say, orientated sympathetically to religion in general but to no specific religious tradition in particular. For such approaches and institutions to be genuinely attractive to believers themselves, it could then be argued that they ought to be justified not in merely secular terms but in those of an overarching theology, an umbrella religious outlook, a "global human theology" as Hick called it,[6] in terms of which all these various religions could intercommunicate and, in good Durkheimian manner, contribute religiously to the onward march and moral health of the contemporary city. That, I take it, forms a large part of the agenda behind Hick's *God and the Universe of Faiths*. Of course he did not, and doubtless does not, see it quite like that. It would indeed be socially reductionist to see it merely like that. The point is that a consciously pluralist theology looked appropriate to the contemporary context, especially to the context of Birmingham. Hick in all honesty stressed that the whole subject of the relation between Christianity and other religions was one he had "largely ignored until coming to live . . . in the multi-cultural, multi-colored, and multi-faith city of Birmingham and being drawn into some of the practical problems of religious pluralism".[7] This is precisely it. As a result of this experience he found it personally no longer possible to maintain a Christ-centered or "one's own-religion-centered" theology. Instead he made what he called his "Copernican revolution" to a God-centered or, later, a "reality-centered" theology. He tells us that "for at least twenty-five years" he had believed that "those who do not respond to God through Christ are not saved but, presumably, damned or lost."[8] "I believed by implication that the majority of human beings are eternally lost . . . this was the position in which I was for a number of years concerning the relation of Christianity to other religions . . . but as soon as one does meet and come to know people of other faiths a paradox of gigantic proportions becomes disturbingly obvious"[9]—the paradox that these people are far too good to be "lost." Hick, of course, went on to reexamine traditional Christian theology, criticize it, and develop his own "human" or "global" theology. But I do not think I am altogether mistaken in judging that for him the theological reanalysis was secondary and that it indeed looks rather weak in strictly theological terms. The "Copernican Revolution," while claimed as a splendid clean fresh start, appears all the more confused the more you analyze it. The overwhelming impression I am left with is that for Hick the revolution was an experiential rather than a strictly theological one. He had previously lived in a Christian world and taken for granted a fairly simple Protestant Christ-centered view of salvation, doubtless more devotional than theological in essence and hardly thought out at all. Entering into a professorial role in a genuinely pluralistic world, he felt quickly compelled to discard this overly-simple and dubiously Christian evangelical view of salvation and damnation and create instead what he thought of as a new "global" theology. As he himself stressed, theology derives from a particular cultural situation. So it is not unfair to point out how very closely his own does so.

This was, similarly, the situation within which new university departments of religious studies suddenly flourished. The university department of theology, supported in the past as an honored part of a national university, itself maintained by public funds, was an appropriate—almost necessary—part of a religiously single world. It existed primarily to develop a coherent ongoing rationale for society's dominant faith or ideology—in the case of Western Europe, some form of Christianity—and hence to service a major public profession, the church's ministry. Theology was needed to relate church to society, and it was needed by both sides. From the 1960s, however, such a department was increasingly anomalous. By theology I mean what it has traditionally meant, a discipline which is not merely concerned comparatively or historically with sacred scriptures and religious doctrines, including an understanding of man, but which does so from a position of faith. With due respect to Maurice Wiles, I remain unable to see how without faith one can have theology—a history of theology, yes, but theology itself, no. A department of Christian theology implies in principle staff and students working together from and within a common faith, though doubtless a vigorous department could reasonably carry, and indeed benefit from, the questioning challenges of the odd deviant. It seems to me perfectly proper in principle to have such a department. In an Islamic country a national university can appropriately maintain a department of Islamic theology; in a Christian country, a department of Christian theology. Indeed the absence of such a department was socially dangerous, the existence of a vigorous academic theology being the best defense against the dominance of irrational and intolerant fundamentalisms.

In reality, however, the one nation/one religion model has long been an anachronism almost everywhere, and the pursuit of it as an ideal in the pluralist reality of society may be a highly dangerous one. In a pluralist society a department of pure theology can only exist appropriately at a more private level, yet withdrawal from the public arena of a genuine university is likely, all in all, to be disadvantageous for theology—though it may still be the right, even the only, option in some circumstances. There can be little doubt that from the 1960s the department of Christian theology in Britain became less and less appropriate as a university institution. Our society as such no longer retains that degree of coherent Christian faith to require and justify university departments of specifically Christian theology, at least on the scale that they had existed hitherto. Nevertheless religion and churches (that is to say, communities of faith) remain an important reality of life, personally, nationally, and internationally. It requires study which is at once sympathetic and scientific, critical and constructive. Room is still needed for the construction of theologies—the rational critique of human life, material existence, political, religious, and social structures on the basis of the faith of significant minority communities. Such a critique is needed by society as much as ever, but it can only be done on the basis of a faith of some sort. As there is no more a majority faith in society, it must be done on the basis of one or more minority faiths. Certainly Christianity in Britain today has the right (in terms of social significance) as well as the capacity to mount a critical theology. Such a theology has no right to a university monopoly, but it has a right to be present there—and as something more than the mere systematizing of an individual's belief. Indeed society itself would be dangerously the loser if influential religions within it were denied the opportunity to theologize effectively at university level and thus encouraged to fall back upon fundamentalism and quietism. The department of religious studies in which all this should now be done is as understandable a development of the post-1960s Britain as is the theology of Hick, yet while the one seems to me an absolutely true and necessary development, the other appears a superficially attractive but over-hasty misdevelopment.

Departments of theology, even where they retain the name, seem to be effectively transforming themselves into departments of religious studies. Most elements of a modern course of theology are in point of fact tackled with absolutely no necessary sense of religious commitment. Indeed the specifically theological element within a theology course in most English universities is now quite a small one—probably too small. This should not, however, mean that it is unimportant, nor that theology cannot exist, even flourish, within a department of religious studies, whether so-called or not. It can. But it does so on the basis of the work of individuals and groups, bringing their personal or community faith commitment creatively to enlighten one or another area of study. In much the same way it is not appropriate to have a department of Marxism, but many a Marxist works creatively within departments of history, sociology, philosophy or, indeed, religious studies. We may note here that if the subject of religious studies is in its scope very much wider than theology, theology also remains in its way very much wider than religious studies. Religious studies is, inevitably, the study of religion—all religion, including the relationship between religion and anything else. But theology is not, as such, necessarily about religion at all. It is about existence in its totality seen in the light of a faith. In the same way an appropriate department of religious studies in Britain today will be in principle pluralist, open to and, hopefully, containing Christians, Muslims, Jews, Marxists, agnostics. They are united, not in faith—as they should be in a department of theology—but in a serious concern with the phenomena and significance of religion in a wide sense and in recognized skill in studying and interpreting such phenomena from a variety of standpoints.

What exactly do we mean by pluralism from the viewpoint of religious studies? First, a recognition that the diversity of religions is a substantial, not a marginal, element within our subject, and that for an understanding of religion, it is crucial to consider the evidence of different traditions (including especially those outside ones own). Secondly, by pluralism in our discipline we must mean the principle that one religion is not to be systematically interpreted in terms of another, and that the department has no overarching principle of interpretations other than that of liberal scholarship. This does not mean that the comparison of religions is excluded, nor even the criticism of one in terms of the theology of another, or any other appropriate terms, only that the department is not committed as such to any single religious or critical viewpoint. I cannot see any other way our subject can or should survive within universities in a society such as ours, however much it may be the case that in any one department all or most of the staff are in point of fact representative of a relatively small spectrum of belief. It seems sensible that in different departments the spectrum should be different.

It was natural enough, in the late 1960s and 1970s, that, as the department of theology turned effectively into a pluralist department of religious studies, and as its concerns with religious traditions other than the Christian grew considerably, there should have been a feeling, an expectation, that theology itself had to respond pretty drastically. In some way, indeed, it had to. The absence of serious consideration in nearly all post-medieval theology—to go no further back—of other religions and their significance vis-à-vis God, the human being, and Christ is obvious enough. The question really was, in what way should it do so?

Hick presents his "Copernican revolution" as the only appropriate intellectual development for a Christian theologian in the pluralist city. Is it? It would be dangerous to imagine that just because a particular intellectual development appears on the surface appropriate to a particular context, it is therefore the correct development, or that there may not be other perhaps less obvious but better grounded approaches. That Hick's was truly in its way extremely appropriate in terms of cultural and social context, I have already tried to show. Was it, however, theologically appropriate? It is, quite obviously, necessary for Christian thinking to change in response to cultural change. Yet it is equally true that Christian thinking can be inappropriately hijacked by the spirit of the age into sudden developments alien to its own proper self. A Copernican revolution in theology can certainly not be finally justified in terms other than theological. This, of course, Hick fully recognizes and his arguments relate to the confused state—as he sees it—of the earlier theology of the relationship of Christianity to other religions (the number of "epicycles" it had, he argues, been forced to develop) in order to justify change.

The companion volume to *God and the Universe of Faiths* should undoubtedly be seen as the symposium *The Myth of God Incarnate*, edited by John Hick in 1977 after three years of preparation.[10] The aim of the book was to argue that the Incarnation, usually regarded as the centerpiece of specifically Christian belief and theology, the key component of Christianity's distinctiveness, was no more than a myth and a myth which today, in "the new age of world ecumenism"[11] could very well be dispensed with. This, Hick's Preface indicated, would have "increasingly important practical implications for our relationship to the peoples of the other great religions." No longer, Professor Wiles observed in the opening chapter, would Christians be able to believe in "the superiority of one religion over another in advance of an informed knowledge of both faiths. Such a change can only be regarded as a gain."[12] Jesus would no longer be claimed as in some way "the way for all peoples and all cultures," but as one of a number of powerful spiritual figures in human history who have taught the world about God. "We should never forget" Hick confidently declared, "that if the Christian gospel had moved East into India instead of West into the Roman empire, Jesus' religious significance would probably have been expressed by hailing him within Hindu culture as a divine Avatar and within the Mahayana Buddhism which was then developing in India as a Bodhisattva."[13] One wonders how he knows.

"A divine Avatar" or "a Bodhisattva." One among many: a guru within a pluralistic world. That was the intended message of the book and one suggested succinctly in the Epilogue by Dennis Nineham. Nineham summed up the matter, clear-sightedly enough, not in terms of the Incarnation but of the uniqueness of Christ. That too, no matter how it is expressed, would have to go. Now it is obvious enough that an explicit Incarnation-type theology is only one of the ways in which the New Testament writers endeavor to expound the mystery of Christ, and various writers in *The Myth of God Incarnate* correctly stressed this pluralism in New Testament theology as, of course, within subsequent Christian theology. Does the vocabulary of the Incarnation doctrine, either in its Johannine or its Chalcedonian form, speak to us today? Does it contain Christology *tout court*? Or is it just one way to talk about Christ among other ways? May we not use other ways? Of course, we may. But beneath such questions there is slipped in an essentially different one: do we need assert in any verbal form at all that Jesus is "necessarily in principle unique?"[14] The Hickian function of the book is to deny it—(though not all its contributors might have gone along with that denial). Now the book's appeal is intrinsically to Christian theological scholarship—an examination, principally, of the coherence of the Christian tradition's internal thinking in regard to Christ. Yet what it actually had to admit—as sound New Testament scholarship must admit—is that while the terms and images chosen for the formulation of Christ's religious uniqueness vary, the affirmation of that uniqueness can be found with basically equal weight in every New Testament writing as in all subsequent Christian creedal affirmation. That embarrassing claim to religious uniqueness on behalf of one man, Jesus of Nazareth, and a consequent ultimate universality of significance, have remained the central characteristic of the Christian tradition, formulate them as you will. Deny the uniqueness and defend Christianity as the appropriate folk-religion for the European West, and you are, I would hold, denying Christianity intrinsically, however many bits and pieces of Christian wreckage you may still find serviceable. Maintain that uniqueness and universality, in whatever linguistic form, and you maintain the continuity and vitality of the Christian claim, however many bits and pieces you may discard as unserviceable.

That seems to me the heart of the matter. Christian theology can only function as such in accordance with Christianity's own central internal logic as a way of faith and of life. That logic is certainly not provable—the sound scholar can tackle the evidence with much good will and not find it adequately convincing, because the claims of that logic seem so improbable. But that is not theology, which remains and has to remain a discipline issuing out of a faith. It is philosophy, one form of common sense, religious studies, what have you. A theology operates according to its own awkward logic, a logic which functions rationally in judging probabilities, seeking coherence in systems, examining seemingly contrary statements, but all within the context of some great basic presupposition. All Christian theology, from the earliest Christian communities prior to the writing of the New Testament—insofar as we can know them—has operated on the basis of this great supposition, the qualitative uniqueness of Christ. No evidence of a pluralism, internal and subordinate to that unanimity, can possibly justify, in theological terms, an abandonment of that presupposition in favor of a quite different religious or secular world view. The attempt of Hick and of *The Myth of God Incarnate* to justify a rejection of that presupposition in favor of an ultimate religious pluralism within human history should be in principle a theological nonstarter. It must also, existentially, be destructive of Christianity as a coherent religious reality. It is a strange stipulation that, in order to enter the age of pluralism appropriately, you must first cease in principle to be what you have been for two thousand years. It is not one which makes theological sense (or sociological sense in relation to Christianity's ongoing community identity), and, equally, it should not be one required by the integrity of religious studies or a genuinely ecumenical approach to the situation of pluralism. That integrity requires, on the contrary, acceptance of the logically noncompatible claims of different religions, rather than the attempt to relate them all systemically within an imagined "world theology," which would be recognized by the believers of no tradition. I am arguing, then, for an explicit dualism: recognition of the quite different requirements of "religious studies" and "theology." For the former remark of Maurice Wiles is eminently correct: in religious studies we must, of course, not assert "the superiority of one religion over another." A department of religious studies could function on no other basis. But such a department operates in terms of a pragmatic secular liberal commitment to mutual respect in the pursuit

127

of learning, not in terms of an implicit or explicit theology of its own. This may seem to privatize theology, but there can be no alternative other than the setting up of a bogus "global theology" as a sort of civil religion for the department: bogus because it relates to no recognizable community of faith.

Essentially different are issues such as an adequate theological evaluation in Christian terms of the relationship of other religions, ideologies, and moral commitments to the uniqueness of Christ, or again the limits of creedal and denominational pluralism within the large historic tradition of Christian belief. The trouble with the Hickian and *Myth of God Incarnate* approach was that it mixed them all up. Such questions cannot, of course, be other than immensely important and their conclusions may well be significantly corrective for the thought and practice of the Christian community. Thus it should in fact be painfully evident that the very simple model of salvation through explicit faith in Christ alone, taken for granted by the younger Hick, was really not the central traditional Christian one at all—though doubtless it had been taken for granted over many generations by countless Christians, Protestant and Catholic. It is too evidently false to the full data of the tradition—including especially the explicit and breathtaking insight of Romans 5 that the grace of Christ has abounded more widely than the sin of Adam. Basic to the tradition was a tension between the every-frontier-breaking-down universality of salvation and the particularity of its symbolic personal initiator and centerpiece. The abandonment of neither is acceptable. Again, basic to the tradition was the relationship between Old Covenant and New, whereby the adherents of both were included within a single history of salvation "ab Abel," whether or not they knew anything of Jesus of Nazareth. Any appropriate advance in the Christian theology of salvation or of the relationship of religions might best start at this point. The fact is that *both* should, from the start, have ruled out a narrow "Christians only are saved" doctrine. It should not be too hard to evolve a theology of other religions and other scriptures, too, drawn from the paradigm of Israel, even if most theologians have failed to do so. Earlier covenants are at least an underanalyzed and underused category in theological thought. But such a development would remain an evolution, not a Copernican revolution and not an epicycle either. This would not be a pluralist theology but it would be a Christian theology open to the full pluralism of human experience and able to build upon a wide rather than a narrow model of divine revelation and the way of salvation.

Different again, of course, is the question as to whether, philosophically, belief in Christ remains a very plausible belief; or whether Christianity is not now a dissolving reality without a future, because without a sufficiently coherent set of beliefs with which a thoughtful twentieth century person is able to identify. That, perhaps, was the true unwritten agenda for several of the *Myth of God Incarnate* writers. A theologian can well come, theologically, to such a conclusion: he or she may come to decide that it is impossible to construct any more a credible and coherent system upon the basic Christian presupposition, and thus come finally to cease to be a Christian theologian, because no longer a Christian. If Christian theology is based upon a false premise it should in due course wither, like many other dead ideologies and religious systems of the past. A theology, while grounded in faith, has still of its nature to establish an adequate and intellectually coherent and convincing system linking together a range of ideas relating to the basic aspects of contemporary human existence in the light of a central faith principle. This Christian theology has always tried to do and often effectively. If it can do so no more, it must crumble. But that is not a matter of pluralism, just one of the intellectual and spiritual senescence of a religious tradition.

It is manifest that an environment of radical pluralism must put a much greater strain upon the theologian, just as it does upon the ordinary believer, than an environment of shared belief. In the latter a scholar can easily tend to harmonize his or her conclusions with public faith without quite realizing he or she is doing so, in a way that simply ceases to happen when there is no longer a public faith of that sort. Such is the condition of modern Britain and such is, accordingly, the condition of a modern department and the discipline of religious studies, within which the academic theologian has now very largely to work. It can certainly be a strain to be loyal to the exigencies at once of religious studies and of a theology. Each, of course, has a variety of possible approaches to pluralism. A department of religious studies will then have to carry along with it an internal pluralism, including a plurality of attitudes towards pluralism itself. Indeed the tension of that plurality may be experienced within a single person. But such strains can be carried; indeed they have to be. In fact there is really no field of modern life and study in which a genuine loyalty at once to liberal and pluralist structures and to one's particular convictions, not shared with all one's colleagues, may not tax one's resources. It is really an unavoidable predicament. People who reject Christianity should not imagine that if they have principles and integrity they can escape it, though clearly some world views may seem more absurd in their scholarly consequences than others.

Today's is certainly a much harsher environment in which to assert the Christian claim to an absolute religious particularity than was the privileged bondage of the European past. Maybe it will prove too harsh and the battle will, quite quickly, be abandoned. But it should not, I think, be abandoned at the first moment that the new terms of service are read out, as the theologian recognizes around him or her a pluralist world instead one of Christendom. He or she should have been more on guard, ready for the moment when the Christian claim would cease to be bolstered up by the claims of medieval or Victorian Christendom. After all, they did not start together. Christianity's nonpluralist commitment to the absolute particularity of Christ in relation to the ultimate meaning and purpose of humankind, God's will for the world, originated within a religiously pluralist world and among its poor, and triumphed in that world. Faced with a multitude of cults it was unyielding in relationship to them. The absolutist claims of Christianity were, one might suggest, masked rather than manifested in their true import by their subsequent connection with absolutist claims of Western culture and political power. Now that the latter have so largely collapsed, as has the connection between the two (though not in much current American ideological warfare, which unites a highly fundamentalistic Protestant Christianity extremely closely with American world power and "civilization," very much on a British Victorian model), it may well be an appropriate time precisely to speak forth the true scandal of Christian particularity in such a way that it can at least be heard for what it always claimed to be—the scandal of God's foolishness, not of British cleverness; of the weakness of the cross, not of the power of the maxim gun.

If the clever and the powerful of today's world have not time for such a message, seeking instead a more socially mellifluous new civic religion (inclusive or exclusive of God, "reality-centeredness," the tomb of the unknown soldier, Lenin's birthday, or whatever), it may be that the poor of the third and fourth world will think differently. Maybe they will be right to do so, finding in it indeed "the way, the truth, and the life," or maybe they will simply be missing out on the most reliable intellectual advances of the twentieth century in pursuance once more of an opium appropriate to their state of misery. In philosophical, historical, religious studies terms, we cannot quite say which is the case. And a pluralistic department of religious studies must be open to all the possibilities. But a theologian, operating loyally within such a department and the pluralistic world it reflects, will still—if he or she is able to stick to his or her last, at once believer and scientist—maintain that the Christian faith has always had at its heart a paradoxical assertion of the improbable, never contemptuous of reason, scholarship or other revelation, yet able again and again to outflank the broader ways of human wisdom and religion with the narrow particularity of a cross, a tomb, a tortured body, a resurrected hope, unique, yet every person's experience. Such an assertion is in some way fulfillment of every aspiration of the most pluralistic of worlds, yet it remains no less committed to a singularly single salvific model, one no less improbable in the first century than in the twentieth, but which for both may still—just conceivably—contain the power and the wisdom of God.

Chapter 10

REFLECTIONS AND OPEN TASKS

M. Douglas Meeks

Not many in the Institute, I surmise, know about my former career as a ballet dancer. As you have seen me walk gracefully across the quad, perhaps you have detected something of my glory days when I danced a *pas de deux* with Dame Margot Fonteyn. But, alas, I can see by your incredulous visage that I am not going to be able to fool you with my wishful thinking.

It might indeed have been wishful thinking when we convened in Oxford a fortnight ago with the question whether there is or could be a consensus on what Methodists and Wesleyans throughout the world should teach (1) within the church's generation of the generations and (2) to the world. Could we find unity on the questions once posed by our predecessors in the faith: What to teach? How to teach? What to do? I think it safe to say that no one came with an overdose of sanguinity that there would be an overwhelmingly positive answer. But just because I have never been on a ballet stage does not mean I do not have a deep aspiration to dance. I believe that even those among us who came convinced that in principle no consensus could be found still aspire that we Methodists dance in a harmonious, if complicated, choreography. It is certain that all of us will leave with a renewed sense of the difficulties of the dance.

Not being practiced in the English art of understatement, I would nevertheless risk the observation that in this Institute we have been somewhat contentious. There has been a healthy hermeneutic of suspicion about "unity" and "consensus." We are suspicious about these words, for we know that they are political words. Masters, rulers, governors, politicians always want unity. In modern discourse about unity we have learned to ask almost reflexively, *Cui bono*? Unity for whose good? We may not have a positive consensus about what to teach, but we do have a strong shared sense of real and potential domination. We have been keen to remind each other of the various dominations that our particular histories and our particular social locations harbor. To say it positively, we are a people who do not want to be dominated and who are ready to struggle against domination as we see it. The simple fact, however, is that we have not all suffered the same dominations.

We have spoken fairly often about being a Methodist "family." But the family members do not want a quick consensus and an easy unity. Who will define the consensus? We have heard several different responses to that question. Certainly not the older and larger churches of the family who are perceived to have lost some of the distinctive aspects of the Wesleyan tradition and to have become lifeless, nonevangelical, too little concerned about personal conversion and sanctification. Certainly not the accommodated members of the family who are not aware of their social location and of the structural conditions of the world societies that make and maintain the poverty of the poor. Certainly not the forgetful members of the family who no longer struggle to remember Wesley and Wesley's appropriation of the Tradition. And so our debate has moved: sometimes at a snail's pace, quite often with consternation, occasionally with anger, but, in it all, as a family discussion around the *only* table which in these times is likely to keep the family together at all. At times we were not explicitly aware of what was keeping us in conversation except the sense that if we stopped talking we would betray ourselves. The final report must be: no earth shaking consensus, no false sense of unity on the question of Methodist doctrine. Gone is any sense of overwhelming theological self-confidence which led a theologian of the last generation to lecture, it is reported, in the following way: "Jesus said, and rightly so." So there seems to be an ever so slight consensus: Methodist teaching should be freed from domination, beginning with the teachers.

And yet we know that something about our Methodist identity contributes to our eagerness for something more: "the unity of the Spirit in the bond of peace." We know that our peculiar Methodist memories proffer something crucial for us as we call upon the Spirit's gifts for "building up the body of Christ until all can attain to the unity of the faith and of the knowledge of the Son of God, to mature personhood" (Eph. 4:3).

Looking at each other across the Lord's Table, no one of us has been free from the burden of the questions, Will our children have faith? and, Will our faith have children? For better or for worse each of us has been burdened with specific responsibilities for the generation of the generations in the household of God. How can we pass on our faithing and hoping in a world that so convincingly contradicts our faith and hope? Do we have anything distinctively Methodist to say when our brothers and sisters in the oikumene ask us to testify in a world where truths are defined by the awesome power of the accumulation of wealth, of manipulable information and technology, and of weapons of unimaginable destructiveness? Will we as Methodists answer at all when the world asks for alternatives to its dominative ways to justice and peace?

Perhaps we are too nervous about our Methodist family. My sense is that we have done best in those moments when we have been less concerned about one branch of Methodism dominating another and more focused on the world, which, as our Lord warned, hates us, and yet which God loves with God's whole being. In a few unguarded moments we have thought out God's passion for the world and have suddenly, faced with the seeming impossibilities of our mission to the world, surprised ourselves that perhaps we do need each other after all.

Would it be wrong to say that in our family what Wesley held together tenuously and at a modicum has fallen apart? We are most separated on the starting point or principal emphasis for teaching as Methodists. Risking oversimplification, I would say that the three primary starting points or emphases most represented in the Institute have been (1) tradition, (2) personal conversion, and (3) the experience of the poor. John Wesley held these together. No one would say perfectly, and yet we would all say that our fascination with Wesley has something to do with his mediation of all three. But our frustrations over our differences about how to put these three elements together are so great that some of us have wanted to desist from even saying the name Wesley for awhile.

Albert Outler's keynote was a mixture of sober realism about Methodist dissensus, on the one hand, and hopeful ways of working at consensus, on the other. As usual, Outler did not mince his words: the Lombard syndrome of Euroamerican theology is at an end. The great epistemological and technological dreams of Western progress are, if still terribly powerful, showing their impotency, except for destruction, and yet are so disturbing our slumber that we cannot yet dream the coming age. The more realistic we are about the bankruptcy of our accommodation to the modern Western traditions, the more the "modest share of doctrinal treasure" we bear from Wesley becomes crucial. This is a point one could have hoped to find more consensus on than we evidently did. If Methodism is to survive the turn of the century, we shall.

Professor Outler masterfully showed how our three questions—What to teach? How to teach? and What to do?—are interwoven with each other in Wesley's way of doing theology. It is certainly not an Outlerian way of putting it, but he almost said that in Wesley, God talk and God walk are inextricably connected. For Wesley, God talk is not abstract speculation on God's essence but rather living and walking in the Spirit. Theology as life in the Holy Spirit is an ordering of one's way of being in the world out of the energies of God's grace; it is "living toward the end of being fully sacralized." A perdurable *sensus fidelium* is created by God's preveniently present grace.

The criticism of theology as a speculative compend has been repeated many times in different ways the last ten days. We have almost reached a consensus: We are all wary of universals, but, again, for different reasons. John Walsh reminded us of Wesley's saying, "I look upon all the world as my parish." A member of one of the interdisciplinary groups related that as a youth growing up in a colonial context he learned of Wesley's world parish while simultaneously learning by heart, "Rule, Britannia, Rule." Bishop Tutu once remarked, "When the white missionaries came to Southern Africa, we had the land and they had the Bible. They said, 'Let us pray.' When we opened our eyes, they had the land and we had the Bible." Whose universal are we talking about?

The Bible does not entertain very many universals. When it speaks in all-inclusive terms, it usually speaks in negations. "All have sinned and fallen short of the glory of God." That is a universal. But it is not a universal with which you can dominate anyone else. The Bible also claims universally that Jesus Christ, the Son of God, has died for the whole world. That, too, is a universal, but it is a universal based on God's suffering of death. It is not a universal with which you can dominate anyone else.

Is all the world our parish? Well, it depends on what we mean by "parish." The word comes from παρα-οικος and originally means the one who lives beyond the household. Πάροικοι are strangers, the homeless. According to 1 Peter the πάραοικοι are those who have been systematically excluded from the household: the household of Israel or the household of Caesar. The ancient word economy (οἶκος + νόμος) means the law or management of the household. Until the eighteenth century, economy had fundamentally to do with livelihood, with access to the household. To use economic language in connection with God and salvation has become strange to our ears because since Adam Smith, and especially since the most important American "theologian," Andrew Carnegie, it has been construed a logical mistake to speak of God and economy together. But the biblical traditions are full of economy and of economic metaphors referring to God. The early church spoke of God's history of righteousness with the creation as God's "economy" and the Triune Community's dealings with the world as the "economic" Trinity. The history of redemption is God's attempt to make a home for all of creation and for all of God's people. The "oik-paranyms" (economy, ecology and ecumene) are about household or home; they are about (1) whether people will find access to livelihood, (2) whether nature will find a home in which it can survive, (3) whether the peoples of the world will find the world mutually habitable in peace.

How should we define household and home? If we follow the biblical poetic images, (1) home is where everyone always knows your name, (2) home is where you can always expect to be confronted, forgiven, put under obligation, (3) home is where there is always a place for you at the table, and (4) home is where you can always count on what is on the table being shared. According to the biblical narratives, God has gone and will go to all lengths in order to create home for God's creatures. According to Philippians 2, this includes God's becoming the "Economist," a household slave (δοῦλος, the ancient meaning of "economist"), in order to create an open household. The meaning of "parish," then, would have been that Jesus Christ is present among the strangers, those who have been excluded from the household. The parish is present where God the Economist is present. Is the world our parish? The Western traditions of imperialism and domination have been glad to view the whole world as their parish. Caesar's household divided the whole world up into parishes, but parish no longer meant the strangers on the outside but those who were within the closed residential, economic, and political circles of a society. One implied question of this Institute has been whether John Wesley broke the hegemony of the Western "parish." John Walsh argued eloquently that Wesley's life in the Spirit made him at home with the poor, even to the point of contracting skin diseases from their beds and stomach disorders from their tables, and this not out of a derived social strategy but because God was at work among the poor building the household in which God will graciously give us all home. "Unless God builds the house our labor is in vain."

For some years now, Albert Outler has been pointing to Wesley's recovery of the Eastern early theologians. Some have remained reluctant for fear of journeying to the arcane. But to return with Wesley to the early theologians is to find a revolutionary view of economy which will quickly take us back to our origins in the household of Israel. It will remind us that our ancient memory of Yahweh begins, "Once we were slaves." There is nothing before that; anything that begins before this memory is nonhistorical, speculative, and ripe for ideological use. Once we were slaves in the household, the economy, of Pharaoh, and Yahweh graciously made a new household of freedom for us. Retrieving the theology of the early theologians thus means that we also retrieve critically their life in the economy of God and ask what implications that would have for our life in the economy of God. Clement, Chrysostom, Basil, Ambrose, and even Augustine will remind us again and again of the Torah, the new economy, the new household rules, the new economic life-style which God has graciously given us and which our Wesleyan understanding of justification will not allow us to set aside, however much the world we live in calls it folly. For starters we can refer to: charge no interest to the poor, return a cloak taken in surety before the cold of the night sets in, leave a portion of your harvest and accumulated wealth so that no one will be shut out of the household and this not as a matter of voluntary charity but in recognition that God has given the poor a claim on what is necessary for livelihood and life abundant and if you do not give what is superfluous to our livelihood you are, *coram Deo*, a thief; resist making private what should not be made private, namely, that accumulation of wealth that gives individuals and organizations power to control the lives and future of others. In the free market societies of the West and the state market societies of the East, these Torah household rules are viewed as quaint and ludicrous, not to speak of dangerous. Because Wesley's life in the Spirit is full of these perspectives on God's economy, we devotees of modern economic instruments consider him silly. Unless, of course, we have some questions about the modern promises of salvation through economy.

Many third and fourth world, black, and feminist theologians in this Institute have risked being strident and recalcitrant because they are convinced that Methodist theology cannot start with tradition or personal internal experience but with the experience of those who have been structurally and systematically shut out of the household, denied access to what it takes to live and work, to have a name and story.

The developing debate of this Institute has shown that no one wants to jettison Wesley. I like the way Bishop Cannon said it, "We've got Wesley for better or worse, and we're going to keep him." But many here present want to retrieve Wesley *together* with a disciplined socio-economic analysis. Why are the poor in poverty? Why does an eight-year-old girl get shot dead by a stray bullet of the security forces in South Africa? Why must peasants in Brazil plant soybeans in their fields rather than black beans on which they have subsisted for decades and so make themselves increasingly dependent on Northern markets? Why did the United Nations Food Council meeting in Beijing recently report that despite a world awash in cheap surplus food, the number of hungry people in the world grew by 15 million from 460 million in 1970 to some 475 million in 1980, a rate of increase of 1.5 million per year? Why are Blacks, Hispanics, Native Americans, and Asian Americans in the rich household of the United States still systematically excluded from what it takes to live and work? What will happen to the world monetary system when it finally becomes evident that the enormous debt of the third world cannot be repaid without a horrendous repression of third-world peoples which not even the Trilateralists and International Monetary Fund have been able to dream up? Are the nuclear arsenals of the U.S. and the Soviet Union even more dangerous now that the United States has become the largest debtor nation in the world and the Soviet Union is becoming increasingly competitive for markets? These are questions that some in the Institute are convinced that we have to work at precisely as we work at pneumatology, sanctification, and evangelization.

Three of our plenary lecturers, Mercy Oduyoye, José Míguez, and Adrian Hastings, dealt with the problem of the church's teaching within a so-called "pluralist" society. Each made profound criticisms of the Enlightenment pretensions of pluralism, another universalizing tendency. Mercy Oduyoye exposed the authoritarian patriarchal and paternalistic teaching in African church and society. She looks for a liberative teaching through communal participation and partnership and finds a model in the Eucharist. A teaching which does not participate in changing the life conditions of the oppressed contributes to their oppression. "For the poor and exploited the future does not include their present conditions; therefore no teaching will be authoritative which requires them to cooperate with such a present."[1] José Míguez questioned the liberal pluralism which prevents the church from engaging in a kind of teaching which takes sides in the conflicts of the public household when it is clear that the truth of the gospel is at stake. Adrian Hastings argued that our uncritical assumption of pluralism precludes our expressing and living the true scandal of Christian particularism in the cross. The manufacturing of a universal religion is simply another form of Western imperialism. To be sure, we need to understand the plural nature of our world and our churches, but perhaps it is time that we stop expecting the buzz word "pluralism" to solve any theological problem for us.

If I am right in detecting an ever so slight consensus about Methodist teaching in our agreement as Methodists to be suspicious about universals, then it could be that we all have to inch toward the necessity of socioeconomic analysis as an aspect of our life in the Spirit. There are two pretentions to universality that are emerging from the first world and spreading with impressive momentum to all parts of the world.[2] The first is the universalist pretention that the whole world can be organized by the nature and logic of the market. We can probably all agree that there are many good things about the market. No country is without markets of some kind. The problem occurs when the peculiar logic of exchanging commodities is expanded to determine the distribution of social goods in all spheres of distribution.

If we stick with John Wesley we shall be reminded that Israel and the church have always known, when they can remember, that there are some things that cannot be distributed according to the logic of the market. We have always known that sex cannot be put into exchange relationships. "Bought sex is not the same."[3] We have always known, when we could remember our starting point in slavery and God's gracious redemption from slavery, that you cannot put the relation of parents and children or learning or healing into exchange relationships, else they be distorted. And we have always known that you cannot put even food, housing, and work exhaustively into exchange relationships without the result being that some are left out of the household, out of access to what it takes to live and work. Wesley did not engage in the kind of social analysis we have to do, but he did know and we need to learn from him that the logic of distributing the social goods that most count for life, belonging to a community, recognition, righteousness, and grace, comes nowhere but from the love of God.

The other pretention to universality is the neo-Hobbesian claim that in order to protect property rights we shall have to give up personal, civil, and human rights. In my country, the Iran-Contra hearings have uncovered various people who seem to be willing to sacrifice democracy for the sake of economic security. This universal claim is spreading frightfully fast all over the world and is producing a growing acceptance of the national security state.

If we are inching toward a still distant consensus on the cruciality of socio-economic analysis for our life in the Spirit, we should at the same time be inching toward a consensus that socio-economic analysis cannot bring God's redemption (any more so than theology). It is true that only life at table with the poor is likely to cause us to break our present patterns of talking about and to God and living in God's presence. But which one of us here is ready and willing and able to live at table with the poor? None of us, without the conversion in which God by forgiving us frees us from our sin; the conversion in which God frees us from our fear of death and the self-possessiveness of life because of our fear of death. Thus have many of us in this Institute emphasized the work of the Spirit, who frees us from our compulsions of our sin and guilt and our neurotic compulsions by which we try to protect ourselves from death.

Life in the Spirit with the poor might give us some solidarity with the Apostolic faith, which Outler called "an illicit faith of oppressed peoples in the Roman Empire." This in turn could give us a fresh vantage point for struggling with the Apostolic faith process. Geoffrey Wainwright made some inventive suggestions about what Methodists can both contribute and gain in this process. Life in the Spirit with the poor might at last help us to see that the Trinity is not meant to be idle speculation. Rather, the Trinity is the hermeneutic of the biblical narrative and of our reading of our present context. The Trinity should be the Christian way of naming God for the sake of Jesus Christ and for criticizing domination in the present.

The problems of the Trinity are as much alive today as at the time of Nicea, though with different forms. The Methodist family will need extraordinary patience to work through the questions of naming God in a trinitarian way, for if we let the teaching of and through the Trinity go, we shall surely succumb to one destructive definition of divine power after another. (Wesley had no idea that lay people should be protected from the Trinity; trinitarian teaching is to be found throughout the early Methodist hymnody.)

The masters and rulers have always been glad to be theists and deists if God's power can accordingly be defined so as to correspond to and justify their power. The universal pretensions to power in both West and East make *use* of "uncrucified," nontrinitarian, noncommunal concepts of God. God is not a radical individual who owns Godself and can thus be the ground of Western possessive individualism. Neither is God an undifferentiated society that can be the ground of Eastern personless collectivity. God is a community of persons with distinct tasks but united by self-giving love. The Cappadocian doctrine of the mutual coinherence of the divine community (περιχώρησις) is still the best thing we have going for a criticism of the racial, sexual, political, and economic oppressions of our time.

So, it seems to me, the path that lies ahead of us is the Wesleyan mediation, through the grace of the living Host who yearns for a new household, of the experience of the poor, the Spirit's conversion of our lives, and the Tradition. In what kind of household can this take place?

Let me conclude by shifting to a more sermonic mode. Things are changing in the Methodist household. That is an unmistakable learning of this Institute. In the midst of the change we should be aware that God is a strange housebuilder of a strange house. It is a resurrection household that God is struggling to build, a household in which we shall all be able to dance, without our inhibitions and our stiff joints. But God will call the tune. In the resurrection household all the household rules get changed.

So it is when the prodigal son returns from the heroin nightmare of his extreme liberal bout with unaccountable freedom, expecting to find a new lease in the conservative legalism of the old household rules. Redemption happens on the road, beyond all best thoughts of liberalism and conservatism, when the father breaks every rule of proper household management. The father rushes to embrace the foul-smelling, dirt-caked child, whereas all power-shrewd people know that he should have stayed in his wing-backed chair surrounded by all of the symbols of his paternal authority. He forgives the son even before the confession is completed, whereas after considerable parental experience I have discovered that one should let children spill all of the beans for future evidence. The father orders clothes, not work clothes or casual wear, but the three-piece suit, but that should have been saved for the highest event of the year. The father calls for a ring, not his fraternity ring, but his father's own ring, but that should have been saved for the older son. The father asks for meat, not the rump roast, but filet mignon, but that should have been saved for the holiest meal of the year. The father announces a party, not your regular Saturday night soirée, but the biggest blow-out yet, but that should have been saved for the celebration of the older son's patrimony. Why all this? "For this my son was dead, and he is alive."

The story does not end happily because the older son does not go into the resurrection celebration. And those of us who are older daughters and sons know why: it is simply not fair that the household rules be changed. I can see the younger daughters and sons shedding a tear for us. But who of us, after all, is not an older daughter and son?

We Methodists stand between the old household in which each of us knows what we will inherit and are so intent upon it that we do not even question the old household rules and the new household which God is building. The invitation to dance is being given freely in the new household. The medieval pictures of the risen Lord dancing, with his cloak extended to include all in the dance, catch the spirit of this resurrection household. Would that we let the Holy Spirit catch us up into this dance. Would that we devote our work to this new household, with its strange, frightening but utterly joyful dance. In a world which seeks everything but home the only unity and consensus worth searching for is that found in the crucified One who nevertheless dances.

AUTHORS

C. K. Barrett

C. K. Barrett took degrees at Pembroke College, Cambridge, and Wesley House, Cambridge. He served as a Methodist minister in Darlington. He became Lecturer in Theology at Durham University in 1945 and then Professor of Divinity 1958–1982. Among his books are *Commentary on John* (1955, 1978, 2nd ed.); *Commentary on 2 Corinthians* (1973); *Jesus and the Gospel Tradition* (1967); and *Freedom and Obligation* (1985).

Brian E. Beck

Brian E. Beck was educated at Cambridge University (Corpus Christi College and Wesley House). He is a minister of the British Methodist Conference and has served in theological education both in Britain and in Kenya. From 1968 to 1984 he was Tutor and subsequently Principal of Wesley House, Cambridge. He is now Secretary of the British Methodist Conference. His publications include *Reading the New Testament Today* (1978). He is co-chair of the Oxford Institute.

Gillian Evans

Gillian Evans was educated at the universities of Oxford (M.A., 1967; D.Litt., 1983), Reading (Ph.D., 1974), and Cambridge (Litt.D., 1983). She has lectured at the universities of Reading (History), Bristol (Theology), and Cambridge (History and Theology). In 1968–1988 she was British Academy Reader in Theology, while continuing her Cambridge post as University lecturer. She is an Anglican, a member of the Church of England's Faith and Order Advisory Group of the Board for Mission and Unity and of the Archbishop's Group on the Episcopate. Her books in include *Anselm and Talking about God* (1978); *Augustine on Evil* (1983); *The Logic and Language of the Bible* (1984–1985, 2 vols.); and *Old Acts and New Theology* (1980).

Günther Gassmann

Günther Gassmann received his Dr.Theol. and was habilitated at Heidelberg University. He also studied theology at Oxford University. From 1963 to 1969 he was assistant professor of systematic theology at Heidelberg University and from 1969–1975 Research Professor at the Institute for Ecumenical Research in Strassbourg, France. Having served as President of the Central Office of the Lutheran Churches in West Germany and as Ecumenical Officer of the Lutheran World Federation, he is presently the Director of the Commission on Faith and Order of the World Council of Churches. His publications include two books on the historic episcopate in Anglicanism and on concepts of unity in the Faith and Order movement (in German). He has also written, with N. Ehrenström, *Confessions in Dialogue* (1975, 3rd ed.) and with H. Meyer *The Unity of the Church* (1983).

Adrian Hastings

Adrian Hastings studied history in Oxford and theology in Rome. After many years in East Africa he became a Lecturer and Reader in Religious Studies in the University of Aberdeen before returning to Africa for three years as Professor of Religious Studies in the University of Zimbabwe (1982–1985). He is now Professor of Theology and Head of the Department of Theology and Religious Studies in the University of Leeds. He is author of *A History of English Christianity 1920–1985* (1986); *A History of African Christianity 1950–1975* (1979); *The Faces of God* (1975); and *African Catholicism* (1989).

M. Douglas Meeks

M. Douglas Meeks was educated at Vanderbilt University, Rhodes College, Duke University, and Tübingen University where he was a Fulbright Fellow, 1968–1970. An ordained minister of the United Methodist Church, he is Academic Dean and Professor of Systematic Theology at Wesley Theological Seminary in Washington, D.C. Meeks is author of *Origins of the Theology of Hope* (1972) and *God the Economist: The Doctrine of God and Political Economy* (1989), and editor of *The Future of the Methodist Theological Traditions* (1985). He is co-chair of the Oxford Institute.

José Míguez Bonino

Educated at the Facultad Evangelica de Teologica and Emory University, José Míguez Bonino holds the Th.D. from Union Theological Seminary, New York. He has since 1983 been Robert W. Woodruff Distinguished Visiting Professor of Systematic Theology at Emory. His writings include *Christians and Marxists: The Mutual Challenge to Revolution* (1976); *The Faces of Jesus: Latin American Christologies* (1983); and *Toward a Christian Political Ethics* (1983).

Mercy Amba Oduyoye

Mercy Amba Oduyoye, a Methodist from Ghana, was educated at the University of Ghana and Cambridge University. She is presently working in Geneva with the World Council of Churches as Deputy General Secretary and staff Moderator of the Programme Unit on Education and Renewal. She was Senior Lecturer in the Department of Religious Studies, University of Ibadan, Nigeria, from 1974 to 1986 and during that period was editor of the department's journal *ORITA*. She has been a Ford Research Fellow and visiting Lecturer at Harvard Divinity School (1985–1986) and the Henry Luce Visiting Professor in World Christianity at the Union Theological Seminary in New York (1986–1987). She has been active in the World Student Christian Federation, the All Africa Conference of Churches, and the Ecumenical Association of Third World Theologians. She is author of *Hearing and Knowing* (1986) and numerous articles on African Christianity, Christian theology, and issues of feminism in Africa.

Albert C. Outler

A Methodist minister and emerited professor of theology, Albert C. Outler was born in Georgia and educated at Wofford College (A.B., 1928), Emory University (B.D., 1933), and Yale University (Ph.D., 1938). His early ministerial service spanned ten years in rural and urban churches. He taught successively at Duke, Yale, and Southern Methodist Universities. He served as chair of the United Methodist Doctrinal Study Commission, 1968–1972. Involved in ecumenical affairs since 1935, he was a delegate to the Faith and Order Conferences at Lund (1952) and at Montreal (1963); member, Working Committee, 1953–1966; co-chair of a Faith and Order Study Commission, 1953–1966; delegated-observer at the Second Vatican Council. He received the Pax Christi Award from St. John's Abbey and University in 1987. His books include *The Christian Tradition and the Unity We Seek* (1957), the John Wesley volume in *A Library of Protestant Thought* (1964), *Who Trusts in God* (1968), and the Bicentennial Edition of John Wesley's *Sermons* (4 volumes, 1984–1987).

Geoffrey Wainwright

Educated in Cambridge, Geneva, and Rome, Geoffrey Wainwright holds the Dr. Theol. degree from the University of Geneva and the D.D. from Cambridge. He taught in Cameroon and in England before becoming Roosevelt Professor of Systematic Theology at the Union Theological Seminary in New York. Since 1983 he has been Professor of Systematic Theology at Duke University. A minister of the British Methodist Church, he is a member of the Faith and Order Commission of the World Council of Churches and currently chairs the international dialogue between the World Methodist Council and the Roman Catholic Church. Dr. Wainwright's dogmatic interests are represented by his *Eucharist and Eschatology* (1971) and *Doxology* (1980), and his ecumenism by *The Ecumenical Moment* (1983). He has edited *Keeping the Faith: Essays to Mark the Centenary of Lux Mundi* (1989).

ABBREVIATIONS FOR THE WORKS OF JOHN WESLEY

Appeals

The Works of John Wesley, Volume 11: *The Appeals to Men of Reason and Religion and Certain Related Open Letters*, ed. Gerald R. Cragg (Oxford: Clarendon Press, 1975).

Journal & Diaries

The Works of John Wesley, Volume 18: *Journal and Diaries I*, ed. W. Reginald Ward and Richard P. Heitzenrater. (Nashville: Abingdon Press, 1988).

Letters

The Works of John Wesley, Volumes 25-25: *Letters I-II*, ed. Frank Baker (Oxford: Clarendon Press, 1980-82).

Letters (Telford)

The Letters of the Rev. John Wesley, A.M., ed John Telford, 8 vols. (London: Epworth Press, 1931).

Sermons

The Works of John Wesley, Volumes 1-4: *Sermons I-IV*, ed. Albert C. Outler (Nashville: Abingdon Press, 1984-87).

Works

The Works of the Rev. John Wesley, A.M., ed. Thomas Jackson, 3rd ed., 14 vols. (London: Wesleyan Methodist Book Room, 1872; reprinted Grand Rapids: Baker Book House, 1979).

NOTES

Chapter 1: Prospects for Methodist Teaching and Confessing

1. See *Apostolic Faith Today*, Faith and Order Paper No. 124, ed. Hans-Georg Link (Geneva: World Council of Churches, 1985).

Chapter 2: Methodists in Search of Consensus

1. Ozora Davis, "At Length There Dawns the Glorious Day," *The Methodist Hymnal* (Nashville: The Methodist Publishing House, 1932), 469; it has been dropped from the new *United Methodist Hymnal* (Nashville: The United Methodist Publishing House, 1989). Cf. the even more exalted utopianism of J. Addington Symonds "These Things Shall Be: a Loftier Race . . . "; this too, has fallen of its own weight.

2. William Shakespeare, *Sonnets*, 73.

3. Langdon Gilkey, *Society and the Sacred* (New York: Crossroad, 1981), p. 13.

4. Carl Becker spelled out this vision of human self-sufficiency in a once famous little classic that I first read in graduate school, *The Heavenly City of the Eighteenth Century Philosophers* (New Haven: Yale University Press, 1965 [1932]).

5. 1920; cf. especially the edition published in 1951 for "The Century of Progress Exposition" in Chicago (1951), with Charles Beard's rousing introduction (New York: Dover Publications).

6. Frank Manuel's comment on his lifetime's study of utopias, in *Daedalus* (Spring 1987), is typical: "Those of us who have in the flesh experienced the sharp discontinuities of the past half-century . . . may feel in our bones the unity and continuities of Western culture. [The notion] still colors our historical apperceptions, but it has long since ceased to determine our thinking" (p. 145). When Oswald Spengler's *Decline of the West* (trans. Charles Francis Atkinson [New York: Alfred A. Knopf]) appeared in English, in 1926–28, it was received with disbelief by all true believers and, presently, the author was muzzled by Hitler. More attention was paid to Robert Heilbronner's *Inquiry into the Human Prospect* (New York: W.W. Norton, 1974); see p. 138 especially. Lately, the trickle has become a flood (e.g., Christopher Lasch, *The Culture of Narcissism: American Life in an Age of Diminishing Expectations* (New York: W.W. Norton, 1978); Jean-Francois Revel, *Comment Les Democraties Finissent* (Garden City, N.Y.: Doubleday, 1983); Konrad Lorenz, *The Waning of Humaneness* (Boston: Little, Brown, 1987); Paul Kennedy, *The Rise and Fall of the Great Powers* (New York: Random House, 1988). This is the centenary year of Edward Bellamy's *Looking Backward, 2000–1887* (New York: Hendricks House, 1887), a million copies of which were sold in its first decade. It would now be safe to offer prizes to Methodist scholars under sixty who have ever read it front to back.

7. This tradition of the idealization of humanity has had many partisans, and still has; cf. Thomas Sheehan, S.J. [*sic*], *The First Coming* (New York: Random House, 1986): "At last, Christianity is discovering what it always was about: not God, or Christ, or Jesus of Nazareth, but the endless unresolvable mystery inscribed at the heart of being human," p. 227.

8. Cf. *Epistle to Diognetus*, V-VI; see also I Peter 1:22–25..

9. Cf. "The Fullness of Faith," Albert C. Outler, ed., *John Wesley* (New York: Oxford University Press, 1964), p. 279.

10. Why has Karl Menninger's question, in *Whatever Became of Sin*? (New York: Hawthorn House, 1973)—posed so plaintively *by a psychiatrist*—been left to hang in the air, especially by our social activists and our special-interest theologians?

11. As in 1 Peter 1:2–8; cf. the important monograph of David Balas, S.O. Cist., *Metousia Theou* (Rome: Liberia Herder, 1960).

12. Cf. Augustine, *Confessions* I, 1.

13. Sermon 85, "On Working Out Our Own Salvation," paragraph 2, *Sermons*, 3:200.

14. Cf. my comments in the Ainslie Lecture of 1984, "Ecumenism in a Post-Liberal Age."

15. A collection of his disdainful hyperboles about "orthodoxy" would run past a page or so; they may be checked out from the indices of the various editions (none of which is exhaustive). A competent dissertation on *theologia* and *theologoumena* in Wesley would be very useful; the times, however, are not favorable for such a project. Taking "the Christian essentials" as *given*, he could give vent to his frustrations with the dogmatists: "Orthodoxy, I say, or right opinions, is but a slender part of religion at best, and sometimes no part at all." *Letters, (Telford)*, 3:185; cf. *ibid.*, 203 and 2:293. "I trample upon opinion, be it right or wrong . . ."; but cf. *ibid.*, 14, "I speak of such opinions as do not touch the foundations." Even in extreme old age (1789) he can still speak of "orthodoxy" as a "religion of opinions"—indeed, as an "idol!" (Sermon 120, "On the Unity of the Divine Being," paragraph 15, *Sermons*, 4:66).

16. Sketched out sparsely in "Catholic Spirit" paragraphs 12–14, *Sermons*, 2:87–88; more formally (and problematically) in the open "Letter to a Roman Catholic," paragraphs 6–12, *Works*, 10:81–83. See also "Thoughts Upon Methodism" (1786), *Works*, 13:258–61.

17. To Ezekiel Cooper, *Letters* (Telford), 8:259–60, Feb. 1, 1791.

18. A prescient call for such a pneumatological focus as an ecumenical resource today may be seen in Fr. Kilian McDonnell, O.S.B., "A Trinitarian Theology of the Holy Spirit?" in *Theological Studies*, 46 (June 1985), 191–227.

19. Christians with an eye to the future might try testing W.H.C. Frend's "conclusion" in *Martyrdom and Persecution in the Early Church* (Oxford: Blackwell, 1965): "The story of persecution and martyrdom, extending through 500 years of the history of the Ancient World . . . still has its lessons today" (p. 571).

20. One of the ecumenical landmarks of our time was provided by Jaroslav Pelikan (then of Chicago, and scion in a long succession of Lutheran pastors) to our Faith and Order Commission on Tradition and Traditions, under a startlingly un-Lutheran title, "*Scriptura Sola Numquam Sola Est.*"

21. As by Theodore Runyon, in his working paper for Group Six, for this Institute.

22. Cf. "Epiclesis," in G.W. Lampe (ed.), *A Patristic Greek Lexicon*, (Oxford: Clarendon, 1961), p. 526.

23. If one prefers better prosody and diluted pneumatology, there is also Bryan Foley's recent "Holy Spirit, Come, Confirm Us" in the *New Catholic Hymnal* (New York: St. Martin's Press, 1971).

24. But cf. David Coffey, an Australian Roman Catholic, *Grace: the Gift of the Holy Spirit* (Manly: Catholic Institute of Sydney, 1979). See also my Cato Lecture for 1982, "The Rule of Grace."

25. Cf. his conversation with Spangenberg on these points, in *Journal and Diaries*, 1:145–6 (Feb. 7, 1736).

26. Journal for Easter, April 2, 1738, *Journal and Diaries*, 1:233.

27. Both the "bated-breath" and the "laid-back" "psychohistories" of the "Aldersgate" experience have been less helpful than was intended. We would do better to concentrate on Wesley's own report: the theme of human participation in the divine nature (2 Peter 1:4) that appeared in his matins reading, his disheartened note to John Gambold in the afternoon, his numbness at vespers (despite Purcell's splendid setting for the *De Profundis* (Ps. 130), the passive verbs in the account of the "warm*ed* heart" (Wesley's only *active* role seems to have been his taking note of the clock-time: "about a quarter before nine")! It has often been noted that the "Aldersgate story" quickly fades from sight in subsequent *Journals*; it has not been

noted often enough that its substance reappears elsewhere throughout the corpus: in the "John Wesley-John Smith Correspondence," *Letters*, 26:138–294 (May 1745–48) and in the two "discourses" on "The Witness of the Spirit," Sermons 10 and 11, *Sermons*, 1:285–98 and Sermon 12, "The Witness of Our Own Spirit," *Sermons*, 1:299–313—and many times thereafter.

28. And, later wrote a sermon about it, Sermon 19, "Heaviness through Manifold Temptations," *Sermons*, 2:222–35.

29. Cf. *Memoirs of James Hutton* (Daniel Bonham, ed. 1856) p. 10; note that Benjamin Ingham was welcomed at the same eucharist from which John Wesley was excluded.

30. Cf. Ephesians 2:8; why is this text so easily turned on its head, as if it read "saved by faith through grace?"

31. Cf. my "Revelation and Reflection: A Comment in Favor of an Apophatic Theology," *Perkins Journal*, (Winter, 1973); see also *The Cambridge Platonists*, ed. Gerald R. Cragg, "A Library of Protestant Thought" (New York: Oxford University Press, 1968).

32. Cf. Janet Martin Soskice, *Metaphor and Religious Language* (Oxford: Clarendon Press, 1985), p. x, 97ff., and 153–61.

33. Sermon 19, "The Great Privilege of Being Born of God," *Sermons* 1:434–5, paragraph I:8, but see also I:7–10. For still another nuancing of the striking phrase, "spiritual respiration," see Sermon 45, "The New Birth," *Sermons*, 2:192–94, paragraph II:4–5, and *A Farther Appeal*, Pt. III, ch. III, paragraph 22, *Appeals*, pp. 305–6, *et passim*. For a safeguard against obscurantism, cf. ibid., paragraph 9. For pneumatology in "the elder Wesley," cf. Sermon 117, "On the Discoveries of Faith," *Sermons*, 4:31–2, paragraph 7; 118, "On the Omnipresence of God," Ibid. 4:42; 47, paragraphs, I.2., III.6; Sermon 120, "On the Unity of the Divine Being," Ibid. 4:66–7, paragraphs 16–17.

34. Cf. Sermon 11, "The Witness of the Spirit, II", *Sermons*, 1:288–93, paragraphs III, 1–9, and paragraph 5 especially.

35. Ibid.; the fullest statement of this *perichoresis*, of God at work in us and we in God is in the late, great Sermon 85 (1785), "On Working Out Our Own Salvation," *Sermons*, 3:199–nk1
209.

36. a. Sermon 117, "On the Discoveries of Faith" (June 11, 1788), *Sermons*, 4:29–38.

b. Sermon, 118, "On the Omnipresence of God" (Aug. 12, 1788), Sermons, 4:39–47.

c. Sermon 119, "Walking by Sight and Walking by Faith" (Dec. 30, 1788), Sermons, 4:49–59.

d. Sermon 120, "The Unity of the Divine Being" (April 9, 1789), *Sermons*, 4:61–74.

e. Sermon 130, "On Living Without God" (July 6, 1790), Sermons, 4:169–76.

They are interesting for two reasons at least: one, they express Wesley's mature pneumatology; two, fragmentary as they are, they share a tone and tenor of a serenity still vital and alert. They have helped me greatly in the bewilderments of my own senescence, but they could be edifying at any stage on life's way. They represent a folk-theology that is carefully critical and unselfconsciously reverent, *coram Deo et hominibus*.

37. "On the Unity of the Divine Being," *op. cit.*, paragraphs 16–17.

38. Cf. Sermon 37, "The Nature of Enthusiasm," *Sermons*, 2:46–60.

39. Note the *pairing* of the two, in his fateful letter to "Our Brethren in America," *Letters* (Telford), 7:237–9, September 11, 1784.

Chapter 3: Righteousness and Justification

1. Sermon 5, "Justification by Faith," *Sermons*, 1:182.

2. *Certain Sermons or Homilies, Appointed to Be Read in Churches* (Oxford, 1638, first published in 1547); a reprint was edited by J. Griffiths (1859).

3. Albert Schweitzer, *The Mysticism of Paul the Apostle*, trans. William Montgomery (New York: Henry Holt, 1931). p. 225.

4. Ibid.

5. William Wrede, *Paul*, trans. Edward Lummis (London: Philip Green, 1907), pp. 122–3.

6. Ibid., pp. 125–6.

7. In Krister Stendahl, *Paul Among Jews and Gentiles and Other Essays* (Philadelphia: Fortress Press, 1976), pp. 78–96.

8. Rudolf Bultmann, *Theology of the New Testament*, trans. Kendrick Grobel, vol. 1 (New York: Charles Scribner's Sons, 1951), pp. 271–2.

9. See note 1.

10. L. Tyerman, *Life and Times of John Wesley*, vol. 1 (London, 1872), p. 443.

11. *Journal and Diaries*, 1:250 (May 24, 1738).

12. Sermon 5, "Justification by Faith," paragraph 4.2, *Sermons* 1:194.

How far may these statements be regarded as providing a universal pattern of what Christian experience ought to be? It is worthwhile to quote a sentence or two of what follows in the Journal. "It was not long before the enemy suggested, 'This cannot be faith; for where is thy joy?'... After my return home, I was much buffeted with temptations."*Journals and Diaries*, 1:250 (May 24, 1738, paragraph 16).

13. Martin Luther, "Preface to the Epistle to the Romans, 1522," *Works of Martin Luther*, vol. 6 (Philadelphia: Muhlenburg Press, 1932), pp. 451–2.

14. Ibid., p. 451.

15. *Luther's Works*, vol. 25 *Lectures on Romans*, ed. Hilton C. Oswald (Saint Louis: Concordia Publishing House, 1971), pp. 274–5. "'Iustitia' et 'iniustitia' multum aliter, quam philosophi et iuriste accipiunt, in Scriptura accipitur. Patet, quia illi qualitatem asserunt anime etc. Sed 'iustitia' Scripture magis pendet ab imputatione Dei quam ab esse rei. Ille enim habet iustitiam, non qui qualitatem solam habet, immo ille peccator est omnino et iniustus, sed quem Deus propter confessionem iniustitie sue et implorationem iustitie Dei misericorditer reputat et voluit iustum apud se haberi. Ideo omnes in iniquitate i.e. iniustitia nascimur, morimur, sola autem reputatione miserentis Dei per fidem verbi eius iusti sumus" (Third Corollarium to Rom. 4:7, W.A. 56.287).

16. "Preface to the Epistle to St. James," *Works of Martin Luther*, vol. 6 (Philadelphia: Muhlenburg Press, 1932), p. 477.

17. Ibid., p. 478.

18. Ibid.

19. "What is New Testament Theology? Some Reflections," in *Intergerini parietis septum (Eph. 2:14): Essays Presented to Markus Barth on His Sixty-Fifth Birthday*, ed. Dikran Y. Hadidian (Pittsburgh: Pickwick Press, 1981), pp. 1–22.

Chapter 4: Reflections on the Church's Authoritative Teaching on Social Questions

1. Max Weber, *Economy and Society: An Outline of Interpretive Sociology*, vol. 1, ed. Günther Roth and Claus Wittich (Berkeley: University of California Press, 1978), pp. 54–56.

2. Published with the signature of John and Charles Wesley in 1743 as "Rules of the Society of the People Called Methodists," *Works*, 8:270–1.

3. On the origins and modifications of "the Social Creed," see Walter C. Muelder, *Methodism and Society in the Twentieth Century* (Nashville: Abingdon Press, 1961), chapters 2–5.

4. The United Methodist Council of Bishops, *In Defense of Creation* (Nashville: Graded Press, 1986).

5. Ibid., Introduction.

6. Ibid.

7. *Economic Justice for All: Pastoral Letter on Catholic Social Teaching and the U.S. Economy* (Washington, D.C.: National Conference of Bishops, 1986).

8. Paul Ramsey, *Who Speaks for the Church?: A Critique of the 1966 Geneva Conference on Church and Society* (Nashville: Abingdon Press, 1967).

9. "Ouvi os clamores do povo," in *Los Obispos Latinoamericanos Entre Medellin Y Puebla* (UCA 1978), pp. 40–63; Eng. Trans.: "I Have Heard the Cry of My People," *Catholic Mind*, 72 (November 1974), pp. 39–64.

10. "I Have Heard the Cry of My People," p. 63.

11. Ibid., pp. 61–2 (translation altered).

Chapter 5: Teaching Authoritatively Amidst Christian Pluralism in Africa

1. Ibadan, Nigeria: Daystar Press, 1968.

2. ACC: African Charismatic Churches, e.g., Aladura, founded and run by Africans. An association of these churches has decided that they be known as African Instituted Churches (AIC).

3. WCA: Western Churches in Africa, e.g., Roman Catholic, Methodist.

4. Jean-Marc Ela, *African Cry* (Maryknoll, N.Y.: Orbis Books, 1986), preface.

5. Ibid.

6. Ibid., p. 6.

7. John E. Skinner, *The Meaning of Authority* (Washington: University Press of America, 1983), p. 3.

8. Richard Sennett, *Authority* (New York: Alfred A. Knopf, 1980), 16–19.

9. I.H. Mosala and B. Tlhagale, *The Unquestionable Right to be Free* (Maryknoll, N.Y.: Orbis Books, 1986); Mercy Amba Oduyoye, *Hearing and Knowing* (Maryknoll, N.Y.: Orbis Books, 1986); George V. Pixley, *God's Kingdom: A Guide for Biblical Study*, trans. Donald D. Walsh (Maryknoll, N.Y.: Orbis Books, 1981).

10. Adrian Harker, *Commentary on Agreed Statement* (ARCIC, 1976), p. 21.

11. Letty M. Russell, *Growth in Partnership* (Philadelphia: Westminster Press, 981); Idem, *Household of Freedom: Authority in Feminist Theology* (Philadelphia: Westminster Press, 1986); Idem, *The Future of Partnership* (Philadelphia: Westminster Press, 1979).

12. Richard Sennett, *Authority*.

13. Letty Russell, *Household of Freedom*, p. 25.

14. Agreed Statements by ARCIC (Venice, 1976).

15. John E. Skinner, *The Meaning of Authority* (Washington: University Press of America, 1983).

Chapter 6: Consensus and Reception

1. Journal for January 25, 1738, *Journals and Diaries*, 1:212.

2. Ibid.

3. Ibid.

4. *Letters* (Telford), 7:54.

5. *Journals and Diaries*, 1:213.

6. *Corpus Reformatorum* 4, (Halle: C.G. Bretschneider, 1834ff.), cols. 664–76; here, col. 670.

7. Conveniently accessible in T.G. Tappert, ed., *The Book of Concord* (Philadelphia: Fortress Press, 1981). In Article 28 of the Augsburg Confession of 1530 an attempt was made to distinguish "the power of the Church" and "the power of the sword" in terms of their respective spheres of operation. The "power of the keys" or the "power of bishops" is a "power or command of God" to preach the Gospel, remit and retain sins and to administer the sacraments (28:5). The civil government must protect not souls but bodies (28:11). Both powers are to be held in honor and acknowledged as gifts and blessings of God (28.18). Both authorities are thought of as requiring obedience, and the issue is whether bishops may intrude upon areas of jurisdiction properly belonging to the state or impose rules and

requirements upon their people without reference to Scripture. The Augsburg conclusion is that any "civil" powers bishops may have are lent them by human not divine authority and that the obligation of Christian people is to refuse obedience to any episcopal order which is contrary to the Gospel.

8. *Corpus Reformatorum*, Col. 670, *partim propter probabilem rationem, partim propter autoritatem quam Deus attribuit ordini.*

9. Col. 670, *non potestas est alligata certis personis aut certae multitudini.*

10. Ibid., Col. 671.

11. Ibid.

12. Thomas Rogers, *An Exposition of the Thirty-Nine Articles*, ed. J.J.S. Perowne (Cambridge: Parker Society, 1844), p. 194.

13. See especially the treatise of 1523 "That a Christian Assembly or Congregation Has the Right and Power to Judge All Teaching," *WA*, 11:408–16; *Luther's Works*, Vol. 39 (Philadelphia: Fortress Press, 1970), pp. 305–14.

14. "Assembly," *Luther's Works*, 39:308–9.

15. Rogers, *An Exposition of the Thirty-Nine Articles*, p. 193.

16. Michael Gaismair, *Landesordnung*, ed. in W. Klaassen, *Michael Gaismair* (Leiden: E.J. Brill, 1978), p. 131.

17. W. Elert, "Lutherische Grundsätze fur die Kirchenverfassung," in *Ein Lehrer der Kirche*, ed. M. Keller-Hüschenmenger (Berlin: Lutherisches Verlaghaus, 1967), p. 103.

18. *Corpus Reformatorum* 24.398: *qui amplectitur communem consensum doctrinae propheticae et apostolicae iuxta sententiam verae ecclesiae.*

19. Ibid., *cui ecclesia dat testimonium.*

20. Lutheran-Roman Catholic statement on the Eucharist, 1978, in *Growth in Agreement*, ed. Harding Meyer and Lukas Vischer (New York: Paulist Press, 1982), p. 212.

21. On the history of consent, see K. Oehler, *Der Consensus Omnium, Antike und Abendland*, 10 (1961), 103–29.

22. Boethius, *De Hebdomadibus*, ed. H. F. Stewart and E. K. Rand (London, 1973), p. 40.

23. See, for example, representing a vast corpus of contemporary debate, Rogers, *Exposition of the Thirty-Nine Articles*, pp. 195, 198, 211.

24. Oehler, op. cit.

25. Ibid.

26. More, *Responsio ad Lutherum*, ed. J.M. Headley, (New Haven and London: Yale University Press, 1969), p. 198.27; Erasmus, *Epistolae*, ed. P. S. and H. M. Allen (Oxford: Clarendon Press, 1906–58).

27. In *Churches Respond to BEM*, ed. Max Thurian (Geneva: WCC, 1986), 1:31.

28. Luther, "Assembly," *Luther's Works*, 39:305.

29. More, *Responsio*, p. 119.30–2.

30. Ibid., p. 191.

31. Ibid., p. 119.21–3.

32. More, *Dialogue*, ed. W.E. Campbell (London: Eyre and Spottiswoode, 1927), p. 182.

33. Rogers, *Exposition of the Thirty-Nine Articles*, p. 193.

34. Ibid., p. 190.

35. Calvin, *Institutes of the Christian Religion*, ed. John T. McNeill (Philadelphia: Westminster Press, 1960), Prefatory Letter to the King of France, paragraph 5, p. 23–4.

36. Luther, "Assembly," *Luther's Works*, 39:306.

37. Ibid.

38. More, *Dialogue* (Campbell), p. 32.

39. Ibid., p. 111.

40. *On Baptism Against the Donatists*, IV. xxxiv.32.

41. Edmund Lechmere, *A Reflection of Certain Authors* (Douai, 1635), p. 3v, reprinted in *English Recusant Literature* (Menston: Scholar Press, 1973), Vol. 126.

42. More, *Responsio*, p. 191.

43. Ibid., p. 193.

44. Nowell, *Catechism*, ed. G. E. Corrie (Cambridge: Parker Society, 1853), p. 11.

45. More, *Dialogue* (Campbell), p. 111.

46. In R. H. Greenfield, "Such a Friend to the Pope," in *Pusey Rediscovered*, ed. P. Butler (London: SPCK, 1983), p. 174.

47. ARCIC A I (16), in *Growth in Agreement*.

48. Wyclif, *Opera Minora*, ed. J. Loserth (London: C.K. Paul, 1913), pp. 327:30ff.

49. More, *Dialogue* (Campbell), pp. 157–8.

50. Ibid., pp. 132–3.

51. More, *Responsio*, p. 626.

52. Ibid., p. 608.

53. Lechmere, op. cit., p. 4.

54. Sebastian Castellio, *De Arte Dubitandi*, ed. E. F. Hirsch (Leiden: E.J. Brill, 1981), p. 3.

55. Luther became progressively more disillusioned about the authority of Councils.

56. Canon Law, 207.1.

57. See the Introduction to the *Final Report of ARCIC I*.

58. ARCIC A I (6).

59. Canon Law, 207.1.

60. Wyclif, *De Ecclesia*, ed. J. Loserth (London: Trübner, 1886), p. 112.

61. Nowell, *Catechism*, p. 115, and see p.v on its status.

62. Article 34, and cf. an important discussion of Melanchthon, CR 4362.

63. ARCIC A I, E1.3.

64. Anselm, *De Casu Diaboli*, in *Opera Omnia*, ed. F.S. Schmitt (Rome/Edinburgh: Seccovii, 1938), I. 235 ff., Chapters II–III.

65. More, *Dialogue* (Campbell), p. 111; Rogers, *Exposition of the Thirty-Nine Articles*, p. 198.

66. Rogers, *Exposition of the Thirty-Nine Articles*, p. 210–11.

67. Ibid., p. 201.

68. Nowell, *Catechism*, p. 117.

69. *Corpus Reformatorum* 24, col. 401, cf. 406 and 409.

70. Wyclif, *Opera Minora*, p. 314.12–3.

71. More, *Responsio*, p. 206.17–9.

72. Luther, "Assembly," *Luther's Works*, 39:308.

73. Ibid., pp. 306–7.

74. Rogers, *Exposition of the Thirty-Nine Articles*, p. 191.

75. Ibid., p. 192.

76. Ibid., p. 190.

77. H. Chadwick, General Synod of the Church of England, *Report of Proceedings* (February, 1985), 16:I, p. 75.

78. Ibid.

79. ARCIC A I, E1.3.

80. Chadwick, loc. cit.

81. ARCIC A I, E1.3.

82. Chadwick, loc. cit.

Chapter 7: Toward the Common Expression of the Apostolic Faith Today

1. *Towards Visible Unity II*, ed. by Michael Kinnamon, Faith and Order Paper No. 113, (Geneva: WCC, 1982), p. 28ff.

2. *Gathered for Life*, Vancouver 1983, ed. by David Gill (Geneva: WCC, 1983), p. 48f. and 253.

3. *The Ecumenical Review* 35/2 (1983), p. 211.

4. *Towards Visible Unity II*, pp. 32–44.

5. *Minutes of the Meeting of the Standing Commission 1984*, Faith and Order Paper No. 121 (Geneva: WCC, 1984), p. 11–21.

6. *One God, One Lord, One Spirit*, ed. by H.-G. Link, Faith and Order Paper No. 139 (Geneva: WCC, 1988).

7. Faith and Order Paper No. 140 (Geneva: WCC, 1987).

8. Cf. *Confessing One Faith*, p. 3.

9. *Breaking Barriers*, ed. by David M. Paton (Grand Rapids: Eerdmans, 1986), p. 66.

10. *Sharing In One Hope*. Bangalore 1978, Faith and Order Paper No. 92 (Geneva: WCC, 1978), pp. 1–11.

11. Faith and Order Paper No. 100 (Geneva: WCC, 1980).

12. *Spirit of God—Spirit of Christ*, Faith and Order Paper No. 103 (Geneva: WCC, 1981), pp. 3–18.

13. *"The Ecumenical Importance of the Nicene Creed"*, in: *Apostolic Faith Today*. A Handbook for Study, ed. by H.-G. Link, Faith and Order Paper No. 124, (Geneva: WCC, 1984), p. 245ff.

Chapter 8: Methodism and the Apostolic Faith

1. Albert C. Outler, ed., *John Wesley* (New York: Oxford University Press, 1964), pp. 492–99. *Works*, X:80–86.

2. *Works*, X:86–128. See also "Popery Calmly Considered," ibid., 140–58.

3. *Works*, V:492–504; *Sermons*, 2:81–95.

4. Geneva: World Council of Churches, 1987.

5. Ibid., Introduction paragraph 11.

6. Ibid.

7. Ibid., paragraph 8.

8. Ibid., paragraphs 11–12.

9. Ibid., paragraph 11.

10. Ibid., paragraph 4.

11. *Baptism, Eucharist and Ministry*, Faith and Order Paper No. 111 (Geneva: World Council of Churches, 1982).

12. "Confessing One Faith," I/18.

13. For example, ibid., I/52; II/93.

14. Ibid., III/180 and 188.

15. See the letter of July 3, 1756, to James Clark, *Letters* (Telford), III:182.

16. Since the writing of this chapter, the 1988 *Discipline* of the United Methodist Church now makes the welcome—and needed—stipulation that ordinations take place in the name of the Father, the Son, and the Holy Spirit (paragraph 432), and the same is implied for baptism by the reference in paragraph 1214.3 to "The General Services of the Church."

17. "Confessing One Faith," Introduction, 11.

18. "Confessing One Faith," Introduction, 4; cf. 6.

19. Ibid., III/191.

20. Ibid., III/213.

21. Ibid., Introduction, 13.

22. From "A Plain Account of the People Called Methodists," in *Works*, VIII:249; cf. the postscript to the letter of July 3, 1756, cited above in note 15 (p. 183).

23. From "The Character of a Methodist," in *Works*, VIII:340.

24. *Works*, X:80–6.

25. Ibid., paragraph 6.

26. Ibid.

27. Ibid., paragraph 7.

28. Ibid., paragraph 7.
29. Ibid., paragraph 7.
30. Ibid., paragraph 8.
31. Ibid., paragraph 13.
32. Sermon 39, "Catholic Spirit," paragraph 11, *Sermons*, 2:87.
33. Ibid., paragraph 12–14, *Sermons*, 2:87–8.
34. *Works*, V:497f.; *Sermons*, 2:88f.
35. *Letters* (Telford), V:270.
36. *Works*, VI:205f.; Sermon 55, "On the Trinity," paragrahs 17–18, *Sermons*, 2:385.
37. *Works*, VI:296; Sermon 64, "The New Creation," paragraph 18, *Sermons*, 2:510.
38. *LRC*, paragraph 6, *Works*, X:81.
39. Ibid., paragraph 7.
40. Ibid.
41. Ibid., paragraph 8.
42. Ibid., paragraph 4.
43. Ibid., paragraph 17.
44. Ibid., paragraph 16.
45. Ibid., paragraph 17.
46. Ibid., paragraph 16.
47. Ibid., paragraph 13.
48. Ibid., paragraph 16.
49. Ibid., paragraph 13.
50. Ibid., paragraph 7.
51. Ibid., paragraph 9.
52. Ibid., paragraph 13.
53. Ibid., paragraph 15.
54. Ibid., paragraph 9.
55. Ibid., paragraph 10.
56. Ibid., paragraph 6.
57. "Confessing One Faith," I/6–8; 21–34.
58. *LRC,* paragraph 14.
59. G.C. Cell, as quoted by Thomas C. Oden, *Doctrinal Standards in the Wesleyan Tradition* (Grand Rapids: Francis Asbury Press, 1988), p. 82.
60. "Confessing One Faith," I/51; cf. I/43.
61. Ibid., I/44.

Chapter 9: Pluralism: The Relation of Theology to Religious Studies

1. John Hick, *God and the Universe of Faiths* (New York: St. Martin's Press, 1973); see also his later *God Has Many Names* (New York: Macmillan, 1980); *The Problems of Religious Pluralism* (New York: Macmillan, 1985), and "Religious Pluralism," in *The World's Religious Traditions: Essays in Honor of Wilfred Cantwell Smith*, ed. Frank Whaling (Edinburgh: T & T Clark, 1984), pp. 154–64.
2. Wilfred Cantwell Smith, *The Meaning and End of Religion*, 2nd ed. (London: SPCK, 1978); *Towards a World Theology* (London: Macmillan, 1981).
3. *Memoirs of Archbishop Temple*, ed. E.G. Sandford (London: Macmillan, 1906), p. 54.
4. Tissington Tatlow, *The Story of the Student Christian Movement of Great Britain and Ireland* (London: Student Christian Movement Press, 1933; H. Hans Hoekendijk, "Evangelisation of the World in This Generation," *International Review of Mission* (January 1970), pp. 23–31.
5. For an assessment of this see Part VI of Adrian Hastings, *A History of English Christianity 1920–1985* (London: Collins, 1986).
6. *God and the Universe of Faiths*, pp. 105 and 106.

7. Ibid., p. viii.
8. Ibid., p. 121.
9. Ibid., p. 122; cf. p. 100.
10. John Hick, ed., *The Myth of God Incarnate* (London: SCM Press, 1977).
11. Hick's phrase, ibid., p. 168.
12. Ibid., p. 9.
13. Ibid., p. 176.
14. Ibid., p. 202.

Chapter 10: Reflections and Open Tasks

1. P. 79 in this volume.
2. For the following see M. Douglas Meeks, *God the Economist: The Doctrine of God and Political Economy* (Minneapolis: Fortress Press, 1989).
3. Fred Hirsch, *The Social Limits of Growth* (Cambridge: Harvard University Press, 1976), p. 87.